in The Tropics,

BY A SETTLER

IN

SANTO DOMINGO.

WITH

AN INTRODUCTORY NOTICE

BY RICHARD B. KIMBALL

AUTHOR OF

"St. Leger," "Undercurrents," &c.

FOURTH EDITION.

NEW YORK:

Carleton, Publisher.

LONDON: BENTLEY.

M.DCCC.LXIII.

Richardson. N.Y.

M'CREA & MILLER, STEREOTYPERS. C. A. ALVORD, PRINTER.

INTRODUCTORY NOTICE.

BY THE AUTHOR OF "ST. LEGER."

WE cannot advise any mere man or woman of fashion, young or old, to take up this volume. Neither the one nor the other will be interested in it, for neither will have the taste to appreciate its contents, unless perchance some such person, in a moment of *ennui*, should be attracted by the freshness of the descriptions and the novelty of the scenes to run through its pages; as a reigning belle sometimes stops to regard, with a mixture of envy and admiration, the natural bloom which mantles the cheek of a fine, unsophisticated country girl: but this is exceptional.

There *are* those who will peruse this book with pleasure and satisfaction. Whoever loves garden, and grove, and shrub, and vine, finding enjoyment in all the gifts of our kindly mother earth, will lay hold of it with avidity. Such will be pleased to learn what Nature—not the stern old parent of our North, but Nature young and prodigal and Eden-like, brings forth in the charmed circle of her tropical home. These have taste and a fine appreciation, and, we may hope, the opportunity to gratify both.

To another class still, this work will specially commend itself; to that class—alas! its members are numerous—who yearn after the happiness of a home without means or the hope of means to acquire one; who have become wearied and discouraged by years of incessant effort and overwork, without any prospect of breaking the fetters which bind them to their destiny, and which are forged but too securely. They will find a way of escape by perusing this romantic, but truthful, narrative.

"In the Tropics" is the twelve-month record of a young man who for a number of years was a clerk in a large mercantile establishment in this city. Finding that without friends or capital it was nearly, or, as it seemed to him, quite impossible ever to accomplish any thing on his own account, and that he was becoming daily more unfitted for any other occupation; warned too by the misfortunes of an elder brother, he resolved to quit the city, while health and vigor still remained to him, and seek a home elsewhere. He gives his reasons for deciding to go to Santo Domingo, and this volume is the history of his first twelvemonth's experience in that island, being brought down to the 1st of January of the present year.

The work is written with a simplicity absolutely fascinating, reminding one of the finer passages of Defoe. The record of his daily routine on his little *estancia* of forty acres is so minute in detail, and so interesting by its freshness, that we find ourselves unconsciously sharing all the hopes and fears of the young American farmer. We are anxious about the success of every experiment, and rejoice at every turn of good fortune which befalls him.

The descriptions of the persons our hero encounters are so vividly drawn that the reader at once feels at home with them. Don Julio

Perez becomes our friend as well as the friend of "Señor Vecino." We embrace Don Delfino again and again as we experience his fresh acts of kindness, almost daily repeated. The friendly services of Juan Garcia go straight to our heart, especially if we take into account the active benevolence of his "lily of a wife" (black though she be), the officious, bustling, and gossiping Anita. These worthy people seem to have taken the "innocent lamb of a stranger" under their special protection, and well do they perform their trust.

To us, however, Tio Juanico is the picturesque character of the scene. He is thus described:

"His dark Indian face, with its gentle mouth and sadly earnest eyes, was not uncomely, and his shapely head, with its mass of jetty hair, was really noticeable in its fine proportions; but both his back and breast had a peculiar and ungainly prominence, amounting to deformity. Aside from this, he was a muscular, well-limbed man, in the strength of his age, and, as I soon saw, as ready as he was capable for hard work. His voice was strikingly clear and musical, but it had the same expression of patient sadness which looked out of his eyes."

Juanico becomes the servant, friend, and faithful man-Friday of the New Yorker, and makes one of the most charming points in the volume. To finish the picture, we have narrated with almost ludicrous fidelity the story of the perfidious native choppers who stole all our friend's satin-wood; then an account of the "man Andres" and his shrewd spouse, who were so sharp in the matter of cocoa-nut sprouts; while the affair of the swindling mason, who attempts to take advantage of the "Señor's" necessities, goes to confirm the old adage, that "human nature is pretty much the same the world over."

But we must leave these fascinating scenes that the reader may the more speedily enter on them. Before we do, however, we earnestly solicit the attention of every reflecting person to this single paragraph. Writes the young "settler:"

"The most manly workers I have seen in this country are white men. Under the warm sun of the tropics, white working men and machinery will yet open the grandest field of civilization ever realized."

A sermon, a lecture, a treatise are bound up in these two sentences. Let the thoughtful reader weigh them well.

It is proper to observe, that we received the manuscript for this volume from an esteemed friend in Santo Domingo City. To us has belonged only the agreeable task of making some trifling revisions for the press, which the absence of the author prevented being done in person.

NEW YORK, *June*, 1863.

CONTENTS.

CHAPTER I.

INTRODUCTORY.

How I came to leave New York.—Why I went to Santo Domingo.—The voyage.—Arrival at the town.—Am introduced to Don Leonardo Delmonte.—A hospitable reception.—Resolve to strike for the interior.—An unexpected greeting.—An old settler.—What he advises.—Start on foot for Palenque.—Visit to Don Julio Perez.—What comes of it.—I purchase a small farm and take possession...Page 13

CHAPTER II.

JANUARY.

First night on my farm.—Happy surprise in the morning.—A singular arrival.—Resolve to turn it to account.—Engage the services of Juan and Anita Garcia.—Tent-making.—Juan assists.—Preparations for supper by Anita.—My new avenue.—Orange and lime groves.—An unnecessary fright.—Faithfulness of Juan.—The spring grove.—My garden.—What it contains.—How we fenced it.—American plough and other implements.—Astonishment of the natives.—The old cabin.—What I did in one month...... 32

CHAPTER III.

FEBRUARY.

A call from Don Julio Perez.—Transplanting vegetables.—Juan's curiosity.—Cutting logwood.—My success in clearing.—Another visit from Don Julio.—Agreeable result.—Washington's birthday.—How I celebrate it.—Anita's breakfast for Don Julio and myself.—My Buena Vista.—Mysterious conference between Juan and Anita.—Preparations for an orange grove.—Juan's amazement.—Success of my garden 58

CHAPTER IV.

MARCH.

Fruits and flowers.—Charms of tropical life.—A visit from Juan's cousins.—What they wanted.—A strange "baptism."—Preparations for grafting.—Startled by the appearance of a crowd around my tent.—The "convita."—My "neighbors and well-wishers."—Grafting performed in presence of a large company.—Pronounced a "miracle."—The great feast.—My address.—How responded to.—José Ravela.—We resolve to make a road to Palenque.—Don Julio's surprise.—He promises assistance.—The road finished.—Ignorance, not industry, debasing.......Page 76

CHAPTER V.

APRIL.

Ploughing-match at Don Julio's.—Stupid native.—Unruty oxen.—An unlooked-for assistant.—Don Delfino de Castro.—Achieve a great victory.—Compliments and congratulations.—Return to Buena Vista.—Important changes.—An "Eden of tranquillity."—A guest for the night.—He proposes to remain longer.—Camp cooking and coffee-making.—Compact with Don Delfino.—What we do together.—His man Isidro.—Beautiful appearance of my orange avenue.—Plentiful showers.—Fragrant blossoms.—Crowning triumph of my garden....... 98

CHAPTER VI.

MAY.

Fresh encouragement.—Site for a new house.—The Mango Avenue.—A "trifling incident."—A rustic gate.—A shipwrecked sailor.—What in search of.—Visit from Captain Ramirez of the "Alice."—Satisfactory solution of a puzzling question.—A market for my vegetables.—Don Julio.—Ambitious projects.—Picturesque scenes.—Twenty-two kinds of fruits on my homestead.—An alluring picture.—An important addition to my revenue.—I hire two native woodmen.—The "New Field."—Grateful acknowledgments....... 120

CHAPTER VII.

JUNE.

Rapid growth of vegetation.—No labor equal to white labor.—What machinery will do in the tropics.—National breads of the Island.—Description of the *casava* and the *arapa.*—Indian fashion of baking.—Yuca and yams.—

Delightful visit from Delfino.—He discovers a new treasure.—A spirited discussion.—Resolve to maintain my "humble independence."—Delfino proposes an October banquet.—Where to come off.—Am greatly surprised.—Visit to the wood-cutters.—Delfino's anger.—An unhappy discovery.—How the difficulty is arranged.—Mahogany.—Satin-wood.—A new cottage resolved on.—How it was planned.............................Page 143

CHAPTER VIII.

JULY.

My palenca.—Active preparations.—Kindness of Delfino and Don Julio.—Manuel, the carpenter.—Description of my new cottage.—A sudden apparition.—Tio Juanico.—Sanchez, the lime-burner.—Juanico's history.—Engage him to work for me.—His mysterious disappearance.—Is he faithless?—Abrupt return.—Juanico wounded.—His distress.—What I do for him.—Cost of building.—The sea-breeze.—Fourth of July, how we celebrate it.—The grand feast.—Yuca and yautilia.—My corn crop.—Abounding wealth of vegetables.. 167

CHAPTER IX.

AUGUST.

A drawback not altogether surprising.—A warning to new-comers.—How I paid for my experience.—Plantain walk.—Different varieties of bananas.—My *Platanal*.—Industry of Juanico.—His brilliant strategy.—Felix Tisada.—Exhibit my improvements.—Amazement of the Dominican.—A proposal.—I take advantage of it.—Overwork myself.—Awake feverish and in pain.—Anita's advice.—Simple remedies.—Juanico and Felix wish to call a physician.—Each knows a worthy doctor.—They disagree.—Decide to employ neither.—My rapid recovery.—Valuable hints.......................... 189

CHAPTER X.

SEPTEMBER.

Famous yield of sweet potatoes.—Contract with Captain Ramirez.—The Captain becomes alarmed.—His fears quieted.—Anita's transactions with the natives.—Cocoa-nut grove.—Its importance.—Am in great perplexity.—Juanico plays the *diplomat*.—Felix comes to my relief.—An amusing scene.—A friendly contest.—Sale of the "cultivator."—What Felix undertakes.—How Felix is swindled.—My despair.—A fresh comer in the scene.—Arrival of Rosa Dalmeyda.—Her mission.—How we arrange matters.—Success at last.. 215

CHAPTER XI.

OCTOBER.

Triumph of Felix.—Auspicious return of Juanico.—His unwonted gayety.—How accounted for.—Don Delfino imports a Stump-Extractor.—Great excitement in the neighborhood.—We muster our forces.—How we obtain recruits.—The process of stump-extracting.—Anita's collation.—Private dinner in the North Arbor.—Don Julio appears again.—Fresh attack on the enemy.—Close of the contest.—The "Extractor" victorious.—Delfino's invitation.—I accept it.—His plantation.—What we do there......Page 243

CHAPTER XII.

NOVEMBER.

Finish my visit.—Delfino surprises me.—We both return to Palenque.—Expected important arrivals.—Anita.—Fishing-day.—"Yankee Charles, of Baltimore."—His history.—American newspapers.—The "Strangers' Rest." —All Saints' day.—Favorable omen.—Improvise a bee-hive.—Arrival of agricultural implements.—All grievously disappointed.—Dishonesty of the "house" in New York.—A warning to buyers.—Juanico and his garlic-bed.—Visit from Manuel, the carpenter.—Furniture from my own mahogany grove.. 261

CHAPTER XIII.

DECEMBER.

The ripening corn.—Hoe-husbandry.—Unbroken succession of crops.—Plans for the future.—Affectionate fidelity of Juanico.—Attempt to finish my cottage.—Dishonest mason.—Unlooked-for disappointment.—What I resolve to do.—Juanico's proposition.—Felix comes to my relief.—The lime-burner.—Cottage finished.—Delfino appears suddenly.—What he insists on.—Preparations for a Christmas-tree.—Everybody to be invited.—Site selected.—The company assemble.—We celebrate Christmas joyously... 281

CHAPTER XIV.

By way of explanation.. 802

IN THE TROPICS.

CHAPTER I.

INTRODUCTORY.

How I came to leave New York.—Why I went to Santo Domingo.—The voyage.—Arrival at the town.—Am introduced to Don Leonardo Delmonte.—A hospitable reception.—Resolve to strike for the interior.—An unexpected greeting.—An old settler.—What he advises.—Start on foot for Palenque.—Visit to Don Julio Perez.—What comes of it.—I purchase a small farm and take possession.

I WAS born and reared on a large farm in the heart of the State of New York, and all my tastes are for the independent life and tranquil occupations of the country. Nevertheless, it was my destiny to struggle for a livelihood several years within the crowded walls of a city establishment, and that with so little success, that the end of each season found me no nearer an independence than the beginning.

I had not ventured to marry on such prospects; but my only brother had loved better, or more successfully, perhaps, and taken to himself a wife. He had the misfortune to lose her some two years ago, and, wearied of a series of discouraging circumstances, which seemed to create, with every effort to improve his condition, only a fetter the more, he proposed to seek a new home in the Far West.

He has three boys, whom he desires to educate in such a manner that they may become industrious, self-helping, and independent men, equally removed from boorish ignorance and elegant imbecility. As a poor man, he did not see his way clear to accomplish this in a large city. Among the cheap lands and growing population of the West it was more possible, and he warmly solicited me to move with him in the direction of the setting sun.

I was more than willing to cast behind me the dust of the city; but for various reasons I preferred seeking a home in some high, healthy, and accessible region of tropical America, to beginning anew in the equally distant, more trying, and less profitable fields of Minnesota.

After weighing all the facts before us, to the best of our ability, we decided to cast our future lot in Santo Domingo, as it had the advantage, unhappily denied to the Spanish American republics, of a stable government, at peace with all other nations.

I volunteered to be the pioneer in the work of finding and making ready our new home, and I set about my preparations without delay.

I left New York on a biting, gusty morning, early in December, and after a pleasant passage of fourteen days, landed at Santo Domingo City, amid the balmy air and bright verdure of a Northern June. All nature revelled in an overflowing wealth of fruits and flowers and foliage. The people were moving about in light summer dresses, and the store doors and house windows were wide open to admit the fresh sea-breeze.

The novelty, and, perhaps still more, the bright contrast of this delicious climate with the wintry rigors of our northern latitudes, prepossessed me at once, and strongly, in favor of this new country.

I remained, however, but one day in the city of Santo Domingo. An American firm there has provided some native cottages on the heights overlooking the town, for the transient accommodation of immigrant families coming over in their vessels. In one of these I obtained a corner of refuge for myself and my few effects, while I cast about me for the choice of a final abiding-place.

A Cuban gentleman, residing in New York, who has travelled extensively in Mexico and Central America, as well as in the West India Islands, had recommended Santo Domingo as offering, on the whole, more advantages to a farmer or mechanic, emigrating from the United States, than any other country of tropical America.

This advice confirmed me in my own opinion; so I followed it the more readily.

Besides advice, my friend favored me with a letter of introduction to a gentleman of the name of Delmonte, who, I soon learned, was a member of one of the old patrician families of the island. He is a notary public, an office of trust and distinction under Spanish law; and at the special request of the official and commercial representative of the "States" in this country, he keeps a list of the most desirable landed properties offered for sale, for the benefit of American immigrants in quest of homesteads.

I presented my letter, and requested his advice. Don Leonardo Delmonte received me with the obliging suavity of a high-bred gentleman, and freely laid before me the details of the numerous properties he had in charge; but none of them came within the scope of my narrow means.

They were chiefly sugar estates, or large tracts of mahogany and logwood forests, altogether beyond the possibility of my means of purchase, but it occurred to me that some one of them might be obtainable on a long lease. I stated my situation frankly, and asked Don Leonardo what he thought of the chances of hiring a farm.

"There would be no difficulty in getting a place," he answered, after hearing me out with kindly attention. "But why not strike at once into the interior, and buy a small farm on time? With the farming implements in your possession, and your experience in agriculture, you can pay for your land in a few years, and meanwhile be shaping your homestead to your taste."

"This was my plan in coming here, but the prices of land seem formidably high," I said, doubtingly.

"Yes, immediately around the city land *is* high; but a short distance back it is almost as cheap as the public lands of the United States."

Don Leonardo has studied our laws, language, and institutions, and understands them like a native.

"What particular section of the country would you advise me to settle in, Don Leonardo?" I asked, after a moment's pause.

"That depends on what you propose to make the principal feature of cultivation," he replied. "We must reflect a little on what—all things considered—is likely to suit you best."

We stood a long time before a map of the Island of Hayti, and, with Don Leonardo's copious notes of description in hand, discussed the several specialties and various gifts of San Cristoval, Bani, and Azua to the west, and of Macoris, Romana, and Samana to the east; but not one of the many fine corn, cotton, coffee, and sugar estates was within my reach, for none on his list were offered in small lots, and I left the office of the polite notary in perplexity and irresolution.

I had turned my steps toward my temporary quarters, to think over in quiet all I had heard, and come to some settled resolution as to the direction I should pursue in my search for a home, when a trifling incident concluded my hesitation and determined my future course.

I was walking slowly along a side street, anxiously revolving my next proceeding, when a horseman rode by at a brisk pace, and dismounted at the door of a tidy cottage, a few paces ahead. As I came up I heard the joyous welcome of wife, and children poured forth in such a flood of hearty, homely English that it arrested my attention, and half unconsciously I paused for a moment to look in on the happy scene.

The wide door opened into a neat, well-furnished room on a level with the street, and a lively party of friends and kindred were grouped around the newly arrived, with the warmest expressions of affectionate welcome. They were all colored people, yet their dress and every item of their surroundings bespoke at a glance easy circumstances and somewhat of culture.

Recollecting myself, I was about to pass on my way, with a bow of mute apology for my abrupt pause at the open door, when the master of the house saw me, and interrupted his account of the state of friends at Bani and Palenque—which, from my recent conversation with Don Leonardo, I caught up with a thrill of peculiar interest—to step forward and ask me if there was any thing in which he could serve me. I excused my breach of decorum by frankly stating that I was a stranger just landed, and that the grateful and unexpected accents of my native land had for an instant arrested me at his door.

"Ah, sir," said the man, in the most respectful tones, "the American language is always like sweet music to me, too. I have lived here near on to thirty years, and with God's help have done very well in Santo Domingo; but there is no treat for me like seeing a gentleman from the States, and hearing of their great doings in steamboats, and railroads, and telegraphs."

"I shall be glad to exchange information with you," I replied.—"The latest news from the United States against your old experience in the nature and capabilities of this country."

"I am a plain, hard-working man, without much education," said Brooks—that was the name of my new acquaintance—"but I have had plenty of rough experience here, and if any thing I know about this country can be of use to you, sir, I shall be proud to do you a service."

Here was the very man I needed.

This sensible old settler, with his thirty years of practical—or, as he called it, rough working-man's—experience of soils, seasons, and localities, was worth more to me, a poor toiling beginner, than volumes of scientific dissertation, fit only for rich men who were able to carry out large plans with full hands. Moreover, he had just returned from a long visit to Bani and Palenque, both inviting places, thirty and forty miles to the westward of Santo Domingo, to which, from among other points, rich in cotton and sugar lands, Don Leonardo Delmonte had called my attention, as distinguished for pure air and healthy water.

Not desiring to trespass on Brooks's good-nature at this moment of re-union with his family, I declined the arm-chair his wife hastened to press on my acceptance, and confined the questions I was eager to flood him with to one or two about the places he had just visited. His answers were extremely suggestive.

"Palenque," he said, with animation, "is the loveliest situation, and has the finest harbor to be found anywhere on the south coast of Santo Domingo, be tween this city and Azua."

"You ought to know this coast by heart," I said, with a smile at his earnestness.

"You may well believe it, sir. I have learned it

like A, B, C, by cutting and loading mahogany, and other woods, to ship at every inlet and landing from here to the Haytian line."

"And what is your opinion, Brooks, of this district for farming?"

"As to that, I can assure you, sir, that all along the coast, about Palenque, Bani, and Azua, is a beautiful level country, with fine savannas for pasture back towards the hills. It is rather dry some seasons, but very healthy."

"And how about the fruits?" I inquired with interest.

"Plenty of fruits, sir—two or three kinds for every month in the year, for the people who will take the trouble to plant them. But that, you know, is the case everywhere in this region."

"Only one question more, Brooks, and then I will leave you to enjoy the company of your family, with many thanks for your obliging information."

"Please don't speak of it, sir. It is such a pleasure to us all to have a few words with an American."

"Well, my remaining question is about the price

of farming land. Do you know how it ranges in that direction?"

"Not exactly, sir. It must be cheap enough, though, for most of it lies waste, overgrown with *monte* thicket."

"For want of inhabitants, perhaps?" I suggested.

"Not that alone, by any means," replied Brooks. "To be sure, the people are not very thick thereabouts, but there is enough of them to do something, if they knew *what* to do, and *how* to do it, for themselves and their beautiful lands. But they don't."

"Yes, I am told the Dominicans are not very scientific farmers."

"Scientific, sir! Why, bless the poor souls, there is not one in a hundred would know a plough from a wheelbarrow, if you were to put them down together on their dinner-table. That is," added Brooks, in a more subdued tone, "if these *rancheros* ever used such fixings as a regular dinner-table."

"Why, Brooks, I cannot imagine the possibility of farming without ploughs, and wheelbarrows too, for that matter."

"That is because you are an American, sir; but you will soon see for yourself that the whole of this beautiful country is in a dead sleep, for want of these ploughs and such like helps to break up the hard crust, and let out the life that really is in the land."

"Well, I think I can promise to show you, some day or other, an American plough in motion, with an American ploughman at the handle, trying his best towards waking up some little corner of this sleeping soil."

On this we parted for the day; but in the evening Brooks called to mention that Don Julio Perez, a wealthy proprietor, a few miles beyond Palenque, wanted to lease several farms on "shares," or at a nominal rent, for a term of years, to American farmers. It had occurred to him that possibly this gentleman would sell me a small tract of fifty or sixty acres on very easy terms, as he was bent on getting some people about him who really understood farming.

I took down the address of this proprietor, and in the morning went with it to Don Leonardo, the notary, to learn whether this property was on his list of lands for sale. It was not, but the owner, Don Julio Perez, was his personal friend, and he offered to give me a letter to him if I chose to go and see the place. I gratefully accepted the offer; the letter was written on the spot; and I went back to my temporary home with a light step, to prepare for the trip.

Arranging with Brooks to forward my effects to Palenque by a coasting vessel, in case I decided to remain, I took my staff and scrip, and set out on foot for the land of promise, the third morning after my arrival in Santo Domingo.

It was a long day's walk to Palenque, but the green and smiling landscape beguiled the hours, and the sun was yet an hour high when I arrived at the door of Don Julio's country house. I sent in the letter by a servant, and scarcely had the time necessary to read it passed, when a slender, graceful, bright-eyed man presented himself with a cordial welcome. I read many signs of hope in his clear brow, well-shaped head, and mellow voice. *Gen-*

tleman was written on every line of his face, and in every movement of his slight but well-formed person.

The letter of his friend, Don Leonardo Delmonte, had briefly explained the object of my visit, and he entered into the details of farming life in the United States with an eager and intelligent interest. I stated to him my exact situation, and did not attempt to conceal the narrowness of the means on which I founded my presumptuous plan of creating for me and mine an independent homestead. Don Julio was not willing to *sell* his land; but he said there was a corner strip of something like forty acres, with a small clearing, and the ruins of an old cabin upon it, which he would consent to part with to an American farmer who would engage to settle upon it at once.

The next morning I arose with the sun. I spent a busy and anxious day running over the land. It was rather well timbered, with patches of heavy undergrowth here and there, but generally open and grove-like. The best point was that directly around the old cabin—a perfectly free space of not less than two acres in extent, bordered by some very large fruit-trees.

Don Julio had named his price—one hundred and fifty dollars, payable in one year. After this brief survey of the ground, I went back in the evening to say to him that I accepted the terms and would like to enter into possession, in order to go to work immediately.

"But this is the dry season," said Don Julio. "From the middle of December to some time in April you cannot rely upon rain enough to bring out any crop whatever that is not put in as early as November."

"But the ground is to be cleared," I said. "Fences are to be made, and some kind of shelter must be put up for farming animals and implements, and this serene season seems to afford the very best weather for that kind of work."

"Very true, there is plenty of work suitable for each season of the year," was in substance Don Julio's reply, "but few in this country either care or know how to regulate their business so as to do the right thing at the right time."

"Everywhere in this world, the only way to win good returns for your labor is to work with system and forethought, and I must try to learn the best way."

"But you cannot live on your place at present?" said Don Julio, interrogatively. "You must secure a few servants, and build yourself a cottage before you can possibly settle on your *estancia*."

"I shall patch up the old cabin for a shelter, and be my own servant until I feel my way to something better," I answered, resolutely.

"Well," returned Don Julio, with one of those happy turns of expression which converts into a compliment what an ill-bred man would treat as a disparaging circumstance; "Well, if you are resolved on that course, I can only say, that the man who has the courage to walk from Santo Domingo here, in one day, to find a farm, and who examines the ground and completes the purchase on the next, is not likely to fail in any thing he undertakes."

"I thank you for the compliment, Don Julio, and will accept it as an encouragement to persevere in my scheme of single-handed farming."

On this we retired for the night, and before my host was awake in the morning, I was on the road to my *estancia*, with a *machete* and hand-axe on my shoulder, to repair as best I might, with these borrowed implements, the old cabin, and clear the small grass-plot around it of the encroaching weeds.

A week later I had planted myself in the old cabin —the merest apology for a shelter—on the land I had bargained for, and had written for my boxes and farming things to be sent to me by one of the little craft plying along the coast.

This ruin of a cabin, the two acres of cleared ground, more or less, with some fragments of the native evergreen fence of *Maya* around them, were all the improvements on the place. Yet I entered hopefully upon the task of converting this bit of wilderness into a well-cultivated homestead.

Partly at Don Julio's suggestion, and partly to aid my memory, when I wished to recall how my work succeeded in its season, but most of all to have some record which might serve a little to guide the first steps of other new settlers, I began from the first to take notes of what was attempted, and what done, as each month came and went in its course.

After mending the thatched roof of the cabin, and cutting away the straggling brush around it, I was ready to receive my farming implements and the small stock of provisions which I had left to be sent on by water. Until they arrived I slept under the hospitable roof of Don Julio.

At the close of the last week of December, the coasting sloop Alice landed my goods at Port Palenque, together with a small cart. It was a mere hand-cart, in fact, which I had fitted with shafts on the voyage, but it was my " chiefest treasure," and I loaded on it the balance of my worldly gear, and walking by the side of the donkey I proceeded with humble rejoicing to my home. I slept there for the first time New Year's Eve, and that night I commenced my new life, and this, its faint, imperfect record.

CHAPTER II.

JANUARY.

First night on my farm.—Happy surprise in the morning.—A singular arrival.—Resolve to turn it to account.—Engage the services of Juan and Anita Garcia.—Tent-making.—Juan assists.—Preparations for supper by Anita.—My new avenue.—Orange and lime groves.—An unnecessary fright.—Faithfulness of Juan.—The spring grove.—My garden.—What it contains.—How we fenced it.—American plough and other implements.—Astonishment of the natives.—The old cabin.—What I did in one month.

I THREW myself in my hammock for my first night's rest in my new home, with an indescribable sense of responsibility, yet with a keen sensation of delight in the free and self-reliant existence I had chosen. But the fatigue of bringing home, and partially unpacking and putting in place even my limited stores, was sufficient to overpower the excitement of my novel position, and I was soon buried in profound repose.

There was no door left on the cabin, and as I opened my eyes in the morning, I looked down a green slope, and through an arcade of waving branches, on a cluster of lime-trees, dotted with stars of golden fruit. Under the shade of those limes, and encircled with trees of larger growth, bubbles a spring of cool, delicious water.

On this green slope, half-way between the spring and the old cabin, I decided to pitch my sleeping-tent.

It was New Year's day, a day of festival through all Christendom, yet it seemed to me that I could not enjoy it until I had set up my tent and entered formally into occupation.

I made my coffee, and had my truly happy New Year's breakfast in the luxurious company of my own thoughts, projects, and anticipations for the long round of twelve months now opening with this bright and genial morning.

After breakfast came the business of setting up the tent. In bringing it with me from New York, I thought to use it for a temporary dwelling on my intended purchase, should there happen to be nothing better to be found in the shape of shelter. It came in good stead, for it leaves the cabin free for kitchen, storehouse, and workshop, and affords me a cleanly and acceptable refuge for my hours of rest and relaxation.

Congratulating myself on my comfortable prospects, I was quite satisfied to regard tent-raising as a holiday enjoyment, and set about it with a zest. While I was cutting some forked sticks to strengthen it stoutly, I happened to look round, and saw a very black and very tall man, making his way through the bushes. He approached with a smiling face and a profusion of complimentary bows, which liquefied, as it were, into a torrent of friendly words as he met my extended hand.

He brought on his back a *macuta*—one of the woven baskets of the country—filled with oranges, plantains, bananas, and limes, which he tendered to me with an air of hearty satisfaction—on the part of his *wife*.

I had to ask my visitor his name, for these Dominicans rarely use any form of introduction, either in presenting themselves or any one else for acquaintance, and learned that it was Juan Garcia, my nearest neighbor on the road to Bani, and that he had come to offer his services and those of his family, if there was any thing in which he could be useful to me.

Don Julio Perez had named this man to me as the most willing and industrious laborer in my vicinity; and so he has proved, for he has worked with and for me the most of the month, in a truly faithful and thoroughly helpful manner.

In return for his acceptable gift of fresh fruits, I could only offer Juan a portion of the poor luncheon of crackers and dried fish which I had laid out for my own frugal meal. So far was my new friend and neighbor from slighting this more than Spartan banquet, that he asked permission to take what I had given him to his wife; and when I threw a handful of sea-biscuit into the *macuta* for his children, he became perfectly resplendent in ivory and eloquence. He assured me that his Anita was a superior cook and an unequalled washer of fine linen, and in either capacity was wholly at my service, volunteering to bring her over in the afternoon to convince me of her abilities in these lines of utility.

These are homely details; but all the daily wants of life press hardly on new settlers, and the ready help of Juan and Anita has been a comforting aid to my restricted efforts.

Juan showed himself an alert, willing, and serviceable man, on this the very first morning of our acquaintance. He had a ready hand for every thing. He gave me some instruction about the value of the noble trees skirting the cleared space while he plied the *machete* among them. His timely assistance enabled me to settle the posts and quickly rear my tent in the selected spot, under the shade of those immense old fruit-trees, evidently the relics of a former settlement.

The ground slopes gently down from the cabin to this group of trees at the edge of the clearing, where they encircle the spring in a symmetrical grove.

When the tent was up, Juan proceeded to cut

some leaves of the fan-palm, and bound them into a broom with a strong, cord-like vine, which he calls *bahuca;* with this *escoba* he swept up the earth floor of the tent as deftly as a woman, while I arranged my boxes for seats and stretched my hammock into a commodious sleeping-cot. This done, I surrendered myself to a couple of hours of noontide repose, and Juan went home.

It was a sweet rest, though I was too much interested to sleep; and with deep thankfulness to our Father in Heaven for the prospect before me, I looked out of the raised curtain of my cool, airy tent through the arcade of protecting trees, and planned my next work.

It was a bold invasion into my shallow purse to engage a man, so early in my career; but that straggling and broken circuit of *Maya* hedge required a native hand to manage it, and I decided to bargain with Juan for a week's assistance in fencing in a house-lot.

He had gone home to carry my munificent gifts of dried herring and sea-biscuit to his wife and children, but he did not fail to return towards evening with his Anita. She is a laughing, buxom body, full of talk and curiosity, but strictly respectful, and fully as anxious as her husband to prove herself an obliging neighbor. Their little girl, Teresa, is a bright and restless child of ten, black but comely, and she naturalized herself on my premises from that day forward. Few noons pass without Teresa darting her round head between the curtains of my tent on some message from her parents, or to ask some trifling favor on her own account, but she is never in the way. The other child, a boy, younger than Teresa, I see little of; and as he is a busy little imp of mischief, I am not sure that I would be sorry were I not to see him at all.

Anita brought with her a cake of cassava bread and some chocolate, which she asked permission to prepare at the fire I had kindled. It was evident they came to get ready my solitary supper. I of course consented, and in a short time she emerged from behind the old cabin, where I have established my kitchen, carrying before her, tray-wise, a piece of a box cover, on which rested some unknown articles hidden from sight by a clean white cloth.

I have arranged my bread-barrel in my tent, where it does duty as a reading table, and on this Anita placed her board tray, and, drawing off the white covering, displayed a plate of toasted cassava, two boiled eggs, a boiled pigeon, and a frothing cup of chocolate. She begged me to excuse her boldness in requesting me to taste these things "for the sake of the New Year, and the poor neighbors who loved *gentlemen.*"

I accepted the simple-hearted offering with sincere thankfulness, for it was pleasant to begin the year with such tokens of good-will from those about me. Besides, however lowly their station, it was in their power to serve or annoy me in no small degree, just as the caprice to like or dislike should happen to seize them.

While these little matters were occupying my particular attention, Anita joined her husband and child outside the tent, but in such a position that she could watch and serve me with a finishing glass of water, and take away the remnants when the meal was done. That over, I went into a long line of questions with Juan about the mode of cutting fencing-stuff, and handling that formidable, long-leaved, and thorny edged *Maya*. This Maya is a bright evergreen and durable hedging material, and there was enough of it to enclose a space three times as large as the present clearing, if it could be transplanted and set out in order.

Juan readily undertook to remove the Maya to the place I should mark out for it, either this month or a little later in the season. Maya is one of the hardiest of plants, and will live even when thrown out on top of the ground; but it takes root quicker and grows better if transplanted after a rain. Just then, Juan was not prepared to make any promises about work; he and his donkey, he said, were engaged in hauling some fustic to the bay of Palenque for shipment, but that should not prevent him assisting me to repair the old hedge, or clear the line for the new one, as soon as I might decide on which plan I should adopt.

Before I slept I had come to a decision. I would enlarge the space around the cabin so as not only to include all the broken line of hedge, and bring in the groups of fruit-trees, scattered all along the whole circuit, but also to take within it the gentle rise on the opposite side of the spring.

This piece of ground I had noticed as a dark, rich loam, free from stones and full of small open patches, indicative of former cultivation. This will give me a home lot of seven or eight acres to put in cultivation with the early spring rains, and with this plan for a starting point fairly fixed in my mind, I committed myself to the care of my Heavenly Father and sunk to rest.

I awoke with the dawn, and hastily sprang from my cot to begin the labors of the day. As my foot touched the ground I recoiled with dismay, for I had stumbled upon a human form, stretched at full length across the entrance of the tent. The figure rolled off the blanket, and, rising, presented the countenance of Juan Garcia.

"Why, how came you here—and asleep?" I demanded in astonishment. "How long have you been here?"

"All night, Señor. I left Anita with the children, and came back to keep the Señor company. I thought the Señor would be sad and solitary by himself, since he was a stranger here."

"It was kind in you, Juan; but I never heard you at all."

"No, Señor, you were asleep, so I only said, 'May God protect him,' and lay down softly on the ground by your hammock, and slept until this moment."

"Thank you for your good-will, Juan; but I am not afraid, and would rather not take you from your family to sleep here."

The poor fellow has in a manner adopted me as his own, and without ever ceasing to be obedient and respectful in his service, he assumes an amusingly parental tone and style when watching and waiting on my wants. He is withal an excellent hand in the work peculiar to the country, as I learned to my satisfaction while we were trimming and cutting away the wild vines and undergrowth under the noble group of trees around the spring. They are all fruit-bearing trees, and now that they are carefully pruned, and the ground canopied by their wide-spreading branches, well cleared of every thing but its soft carpet of "velvet grass," the "SPRING GROVE," as I am proud to call it, is a noble feature in my home landscape. I did not know the value of this magnificent group of trees until Juan informed me that morning what they all were. He particularly called my attention to two of them, loaded with round green fruit, which he told me was the famous *caimete.* This fruit ripens early in February, and holds on through all March, and sometimes deep into April. Its rich, delicious pulp has been happily compared to "peaches crushed in cream." From the two or three which I have already enjoyed, for mine are now ripening, I think this delicate fruit deserves all the praise lavished upon it.

Stimulated by the happy discovery that it was a superb fruit-grove, instead of a cluster of wild forest trees, which shades my tent and the beautiful spring slope before it, I could hardly keep to the rule I had laid down, to quit hard out-door work at eleven. Juan worked with me at clearing with steady good-will, cutting away the brush, lopping off the dead limbs, and piling up the trash for burning; and between us we had given a different aspect to the Spring Grove, and to the green borders of the spring itself, before we left them.

Juan carried home his share of my plain dinner, and after his departure I sought my hammock for an hour of rest and reflection. I wanted to consider what I should do first of all in the way of providing for my support when the stock of provisions should be exhausted. It is the dry season, and *crops*, that is to say, products in quantities intended for sale, could not be started at this time of year. Whatever was already a month in the ground, and well under way, so that the roots could find a little moisture below the surface, would keep on growing and ripening.

"Oh, that I had come out in October," I thought. "Had I been here with the fall rains, I might have had, at least, a vegetable garden very well advanced."

Then arose the question:—"But may I not even now prepare and sow a bed with a part of the seeds I brought with me? By dint of care and watering, can I not gain a month or two on the dry season, and raise a few vegetables for my own table?" As I asked myself these things, I was answered in my own mind that it was well worth the experiment.

Yes, I would start a seedling bed without delay, and before the seeds were out of the ground, Juan and I might have the old fence so far repaired that I need fear nothing for my young plants. I could not remain in my hammock after this idea seized me. I was anxious to begin, and besides, the site I had selected would be partially in the shade, and pleasant for work early in the afternoon.

Before two o'clock, my hour for commencing the afternoon labors, I had got my tools ready and had marked off a bed ten feet long and four wide, on the east side of the old cabin. On the west side is my kitchen, and the south looks towards my tent. I chose the east to give it the benefit of the morning sun, and yet secure it some shelter from the scorch ing afternoons. With my pick-axe, hoe, and rake, I had managed to get this rich bit of ground in pretty thorough tilth when Juan and his wife dropped in upon me, about five o'clock in the afternoon. Their amazement was almost beyond words. "To work in the dry season! To work so much on such a little bit of ground. To work with so many tools." They both stood and rung the changes on these singular innovations upon their mode of cultivation, until they were out of breath.

Juan took my want of experience in serious compassion.

"Do you know, Señor," he asked, impressively, "that in our climate nothing you plant in the dry season bears fruit until the rains come on, unless you water it many, many times?"

"But I intend to water what I sow in this bed as often and as much as is necessary to bring the plants forward. I want to eat of these vegetables two months earlier than I can have them if I wait for the settled rains."

"But do they take so much trouble in your country to have a few young beans and tomatoes in March when you can have them without any trouble in May?" asked Juan, in undisguised wonder at such absurd practices.

"Why not, Juan? We can have nothing in this world without trouble and sacrifice."

Juan and Anita were by no means convinced of the wisdom of my course, but they very cheerfully brought water from the spring and gave the seedling bed a plentiful bath, while I put in the little rows of ocra, onion, tomato, and egg-plant destined for future transplantation, alternated by like rows of lettuce and radishes, which are to remain in final possession of the ground they now occupy until called to the table.

By the time all the seed was duly covered in the little rows, and I had finished off the bed with a row of "early bush beans" at the outside edge, it was dusk, and Anita called me to a pleasant supper of her own arrangement. While the supper and the seedling bed were simultaneously receiving the last touches of preparation, Anita, who had become intensely interested in both, kept running from one to the other in an amusing flurry of haste and excitement.

"Ah, Maria Purissima! what a variety of seeds, and all marked out in such order. Will it please the Señor to come to supper? The rice cooked in cocoa-milk is perfectly ready. But to think of seven kinds of vegetables, all set in beautiful rows like the seven cardinal virtues, and the whole to be fed with water through the dry season. Wonderful! wonderful!"

Anita's distribution of the "seven cardinal virtues" was as incomprehensible to my understanding, as my disposition of the seven vegetables seemed to hers; but not choosing to expose my ignorance, I went into supper without asking any questions.

After Juan and Anita had attended to theirs, we held a council on the condition of the fences, and the propriety of immediately clearing a few more acres of land, for the double purpose of enlarging my planting space, and of obtaining a supply of wood to enclose it.

In conclusion, Juan agreed to work for me four days in the week for the next six or eight weeks, at half a dollar a day. He reserved two days in the week for his own clearing and planting, which he said he should conduct partly on the native plan and partly on mine, for he wanted to learn "American ways," and, most of all, the use of the "Yankee" plough, of which he had heard surprising things from persons who had seen it tearing up the ground in Cuba and Porto Rico.

Finally, assuring me that I could depend upon his coming to me with the sun the next day, Juan and his wife went to their home, and left me to my solitary slumbers.

Juan was faithful to his word, and the work of fencing in the space intended for the Home Field was begun in earnest. Two sides—those forming the line of my property on the north and west—are to be guarded by a Maya hedge and were left for the last. The other two sides will be partition fences, if I am fortunate enough to carry out my present plans, and those we have closed in with a *palisar* or stake fence.

A Dominican palisar is a very simple, yet, if well made, a very effective affair. Stout stakes are driven firmly into the earth at short intervals, and crossbars are woven in and bound to them with strong and durable vine-stems, which are called *bahuca.*

As fast as Juan and I cleared the ground we laid up the posts and bars, and bahuca, and collected all the brush, which was too small for service, in heaps for burning.

The last week of the month, Juan and half a dozen boys, whom he had collected from I know not where, made a perfect holiday of bonfires of it, and my first field stands almost ready for planting. There still remains a strip of tangled undergrowth where the old fence ran, but it is a perfect nursery of young fruit-trees, which I wish to trim out and transplant when the season permits. January is the month of months for cutting timber and clearing new ground for crops, and it has been fully occupied with its appropriate work.

There were three very heavy rains in the early part of the month, and under their favor I made a melon-patch back of the old cabin, and a much larger one by the spring, of the savory Dominican *calabazas.*

They are all thriving, and so is a triple row of pole beans on each side of the path to the spring.

Anita comes over every day or two to admire the progress of the seedling bed, which is now well advanced, and to count up what varieties of vegetables I have under way. She has herself smuggled parsley, thyme, and coriander seeds among my beans, and reckons them up with the melons among the *vegetables*. She proposes to make a "superb soup" for Easter Monday, in which they are all to figure, I believe,—melons, cucumbers, and coriander included.

Now, at the close of the month, I can fully realize how fortunate it has been for me that I began my farming experience in Santo Domingo in the serene month of January. It is really the first month of the "dry season," though that is reckoned to begin with December. These are the two best months for beginners from the North. At this season the heavy rains of the summer and early fall sensibly diminish in force, and before February sets in they cease almost entirely, leaving an interval of from seven to nine weeks of bright weather, scarcely interrupted by a passing shower, which the settler should not fail to take advantage of.

This secure period of calm and cloudless sky has given me time to form my plans, to select and clear my planting-ground, and to strengthen my fences against my neighbor's cattle; I have none of my own as yet, to fence in or out.

CHAPTER III.

FEBRUARY.

A call from Don Julio Perez.—Transplanting vegetables.—Juan's curiosity.—Cutting logwood.—My success in clearing.—Another visit from Don Julio.—Agreeable result.—Washington's birthday.—How I celebrate it.—Anita's breakfast for Don Julio and myself.—My Buena Vista.—Mysterious conference between Juan and Anita.—Preparations for an orange grove.—Juan's amazement.—Success of my garden.

WE were blessed with a rainy week in the early part of the month, and under favor of this unusual refreshment of the earth, in the heart of the dry season, I made a kind of winter garden at the low, moist margin of the spring. In the rainy season this bit of low ground, at the outlet of this precious, unfailing fountain, might be altogether too wet for satisfactory cultivation; but in the period of drought it offers the only spot on my little homestead on which I can securely rely for a fresh succession of the more delicate vegetables through most of January, February, and March.

The morning after the first fall of rain I was up with the dawn, and at work in my projected "winter garden," breaking up the ground and laying off the plats in regular order for the various plantings.

"You are at work early, sir," said a voice at my elbow, as I was wielding the pick-axe with all the vigor of the fresh morning. I looked up in surprise, and met the kindly smile and extended hand of Don Julio Perez.

"I rode over to see your improvements, *vecino mio*," said Don Julio, "and more particularly to warn you that it is not safe for an unacclimated person, like yourself, to continue your labors through the heat of the day."

"Thank you, Don Julio, for your consideration, but that is precisely what I am careful not to do," I answered. "I abstain from all severe out-door labor after ten—or, at the latest, eleven—in the morning, and do not resume it again until two or three in the afternoon."

"And yet, the five weeks you have been here have left their mark," said Don Julio, politely, as he led his horse a few steps up the spring slope, and swept the clearing, of which it was the centre, with a look of mingled curiosity and satisfaction. "This large clearing speaks strongly of an American axe in American hands."

"I have a faithful help in Juan Garcia," I observed, "and in the hours I dedicate to labor I feel able to work to some purpose."

"Perhaps it would be better for us all, natives as well as foreigners, not to exhaust our energies at mid-day," resumed Don Julio, after a moment of thoughtful silence.

"*I* find it well, at least, I assure you, and I would extend the rule in some degree to Juan, but he cannot be kept to the early morning hours of labor which I prescribe to myself."

"Of course not," said Don Julio; "none of these people will give you a fair day's work, except in their own old way. But the cool morning is running away, and I am detaining you: Adios."

Springing on his horse, Don Julio galloped off almost as abruptly as he came, but not without pressing upon me the offer of a yoke or two of oxen to plough up my corn-land in its season.

To return to my February rains, and their results. The seedling bed of January, nursed with many copious waterings, became so thick set that it was necessary to transplant freely to give room for growth. Juan went on alone with the Maya hedge, setting that in its place with his native bush-hook, while I set out abundance of tomatoes, egg-plant, ocra, and other vegetables in my winter garden. We both made the most of our plants while the earth was moist with recent showers. They have taken very well, and Juan brings over his friends every now and then to see and wonder at the extraordinary trouble I have taken "to have things grow in spite of the *seco*—dry season."

Nevertheless, Juan and I are visibly progressing with our clearing and fencing arrangements, and our enlarged lot is now, at the last of the month, ready for the plough, where the stumps will permit it to pass. Burning the brush has killed them off, and will prevent "sprouting," and I have promised Juan that by the close of the rainy season—or whenever the care of the crop will best allow it—we will rig out a stump-puller with our ox-chain, and make clean work of most of the ground. He is wild with curiosity to see the process of drawing out roots, as I have compared it to extracting teeth.

February, with its almost unbroken succession of calm, summer-like days, is exactly fitted to the business of clearing, and more can be done in one such week, than in two when the rains set in; besides, the time of rains should be employed in planting the ground duly made ready in advance, when little else can be done.

February is also a good month for pruning and grafting, except for such trees as are then in the midst of their fruit-bearing.

In the morning, after devoting an hour to my vegetables and fruit-trees, Juan would present himself for work and his breakfast—a camp breakfast of the roughest, but perfectly acceptable to a healthy appetite. Then to our daily war on the woodlands—I with my keen, smooth-helved American axe, to fell the trees during my appointed hours of toil, and Juan to trim off the branches with his long-bladed native *machete*—always taking care as we went on to pile aside the fence-stakes, and heap up the useless brush for burning, as we had been doing through January.

There was a beautiful eminence—a round knoll, crowned with a dense grove of logwood, sloping upward from the farther margin of the spring—which gave us no little toil and trouble. It was a thorny tanglement of undergrowth terrible to attack, but we persevered with axe, *machete*, and brush-hook, until it was all brought to the ground, and the logwood trimmed for market.

One bright afternoon Don Julio dropped down upon us in his sudden way, just as we were piling up the last of our logwood, and inquired what I intended doing with it. I knew it was a marketable commodity, and that Don Julio was a large exporter of mahogany and other woods; so I replied, half in jest, half in earnest, that I proposed to sell it to him in part payment of my land.

"But you are not called upon to pay me any thing before the end of the year," said Don Julio.

"Nevertheless, I would gladly dispose of this logwood as it lies here, and cancel so much of my indebtedness as it will cover. I leave the price to yourself, Don Julio, as you are experienced in woods, if you choose to take it."

Don Julio dismounted with a smile, and examined the logwood—*Campeche*, it is called here—with attention.

"This is a fine lot, and convenient to the landing, and at ten dollars a ton may be fairly worth one hundred dollars," he said, as he remounted his horse. "I will allow you that sum as it lies; or, if you prefer, you may take it to the scales at Port Palenque landing, and I will pay you by its weight ten dollars the ton."

"I accept the hundred dollars, Don Julio. The logwood is yours, and," I added to myself, with a bounding heart, "two-thirds of the purchase price of this fair homestead has been won from it in less than two months' occupation."

This was the 21st of February, and on the 22d I kept holiday, in memory of the birth of Washington.

It was a day of twofold interest,—dear in memory of the Father of his country, and dear because it saw me in very deed the owner of my homestead. At my request Anita came early, to prepare a camp breakfast, for Don Julio had promised to ride over in the morning with the papers for my land, and take a cup of coffee with me. Of course, there was no end of bustle and anxiety of preparation from sunrise to about ten, when our guest presented himself, and the table was served with fresh lettuce, rosy radishes, crisp cucumbers, and green beans. These first-fruits of my industry figured, in this melange of all meals, with the fresh cassava, nice *calabaza*, sweet potatoes, and other vegetables from Juan's patch of garden, besides a brace of broiled pigeons and a gourdshell of boiled eggs as central ornaments. Not the least luxury, in my estimation, was a plate of peachy-pulped caimetes, and another of the rosy, sub-acid pomegranate, mingled with creamy custard apples, all from my own trees. The oranges were from Juan's cottage door—I have none as yet—but all the other fruits were from the grand old trees around the spring.

It was an odd, but abundant, and not unsavory meal, yet there was not an article upon our rustic table that came from the United States, except the toasted sea-biscuit and the Orange County butter that dressed it.

The corn and the cassava bread were the product of Juan's labor, but the coffee and sugar came from Don Julio's plantation. His kind and neighborly old *mayoral*—land steward—had proposed an exchange of those articles for some of my salted stores, and both of us have found the arrangement satisfactory.

This trifling matter is only worthy of note because other new settlers may find it convenient to be instructed by it. My first entertainment under the shelter of my own tent was, therefore, in nowise an

American affair. It was Dominican—thoroughly and amusingly Dominican—in all its details. The ruling idea was quantity. Every available nook and shelf was put in requisition to hold some portion of Anita's elaborate display; but the coffee was good, the omelet respectable, the *picadia* excellent, and the pigeons delicious, so that ample justice was done to the extraordinary efforts of Juan and his wife.

After coffee, we took our oranges and our cigars under the shade of the superb trees overhanging the spring slope, and left the tent and their share of the breakfast to these willing servants, for a quiet hour of enjoyment in *their* way.

Meanwhile, Don Julio delivered to me the title-deeds of my place, duly attested in legal form. They had been made out as if the money were all paid, and he almost refused to take the note I had written for the balance due him.

In his desire to serve me, he suggested the superior profits to be gained by cutting mahogany, satin-wood, *Campeche*, ship-timber, etc., and offered me liberal conditions if I felt disposed to procure a good force of axemen and teamsters from the United States, and take charge of a valuable tract of forest owned by him near the Haytien frontier. I declined, partly on the plea of my insufficient capital and experience for such an undertaking; but the stronger reason, as I frankly informed him, was my uncontrollable desire to obtain a settled and immediate home for me and mine.

"Perhaps you are right. Yes, I have no doubt of it, my friend," said Don Julio, after one of his thoughtful pauses. "Health, tranquillity, and independence are the greatest of earthly blessings, and you are now on the surest road to them."

Throwing away the stump of his cigar, he arose and sauntered through my cherished and thriving winter garden, complimenting the arrangement of the beds, and promising to send me plenty of ginger and arrow-root to edge the borders, and also bespeaking a supply of tomatoes and ocra for his own table.

These plants are setting in fruit and blossom, and there will be an over supply for us all, if they yield as well as they promise.

Returning from this circuit, Don Julio called for his horse, but, with the bridle over his arm, he lingered and chatted over farming matters as he slowly ascended, the knoll where he had found us piling logwood the previous day. I was walking beside him when he stopped abruptly, and exclaimed with enthusiasm:

"What a lovely prospect! How is it that I never saw it before?"

I glanced round in surprise. Then, for the first time, from the summit of the knoll lately occupied by the *Campeche* grove, I caught an indistinct but charming view of the blue and dancing sea. It was seen in broken glimpses through the intervening trunks of forest-trees, and only a narrow belt of foliage, easily swept away, marred the wide prospect. The dense chapparal had hitherto completely obscured the beautiful reach of lower land and the swelling waves beyond it; but the last labors of Juan the day before had rent away the veil. Until that moment I had no idea that this moderate elevation commanded such an extensive view. I observed to Don Julio, after we had gazed awhile in silence on its unexpected beauties—

"But it surprises me that you, the owner of this estate, should not have known it before."

"I was aware," he replied, "that in old times there was a residence here called Buena Vista—Fine View—yet it never occurred to me to ask why. But hark! is not that the murmur of the surf?"

"Yes, undoubtedly it is," I said, after listening a moment, "and distinct enough, too. It is singular that in all the last week, while Juan and I were cutting this timber, neither of us noticed the sound of the surf."

"Not at all. The wind did not happen to set this way, and the rustle of the falling trees would deaden the sound."

"Then these magnificent old fruit-trees, which I am taking such a delight in pruning, were perhaps planted for the adornment of Buena Vista?" I suggested.

"Undoubtedly," replied Don Julio. "And now I recollect that some of the old men about here have told, me that in the days of its splendor this estate had a straight avenue, with a double line of orange-trees on each side of it, from the mansion to Port Palenque. The orange-trees were choked to death long ago, but my people may find the line of the old road when they take this logwood down to the landing."

"I too will look out for it, Don Julio, and be assured I shall exert myself to do all that Juan's labor and mine can help towards opening a direct road to the landing. The winding mule-path we are using now is a rough affair."

"Do so, *vecino mio*," replied Don Julio, with a farewell grasp of the hand, "and we will also talk about what can be done in the way of extending your boundaries in that direction if you require more land."

After his departure I threw myself on the ground under the shade of the interlacing branches of the noble fruit-trees—which I now felt were so really my own—and thought over the cheering success of my single-handed search for a home.

I was still buried in these pleasant reveries when Juan broke into them by bringing me a *caimete* branch, loaded with that most delicious fruit. He asked me if I was sick, that I remained so long sitting motionless under a tree, neither eating, sleeping, nor smoking. I answered by pointing to the snatches of blue sea visible through the trees. He threw a careless glance in that direction and asked me if I thought the sea as beautiful as the savanna.

"Sea and savanna are equally beautiful, Juan, each in its way; but this grand reach of blue waves and the fresh and bracing air which they will send to us every hour of our lives are alone worth all I have paid for this *estancia*. I hope to build my own dwelling on this old site of Buena Vista, if it shall please our Heavenly Father to smile on my efforts in Santo Domingo."

Juan was astonished at the value I set on a sea view, and assured me that he had at his *rancho* almost as wide a prospect, but that a few bushes, which he had never thought of taking the trouble to cut away, had grown up and hid it from sight.

He could partly appreciate the care I was bestowing on the fruit-trees; he liked fruit himself, if it was to be had without much trouble; and the shade was rather agreeable in the lazy noon-tide; but the superfluity of a graceful arrangement or the charms of an extensive prospect were below, or beyond, his consideration.

When we returned to the tent he shared his surprise with his wife, and he made the computation in his own fashion when he stated to her how highly the Señor valued his sea prospect. He had assisted in cutting down the logwood that covered the old site, and was present when I sold it to Don Julio, and he spoke, therefore, as one having official information.

"Anita, my lily, would you believe it," he said to her confidentially, while I was out of sight, but not out of hearing, mixing a glass of fresh lemonade within the curtains of my tent, "would you believe it, Señor Vecino says, very positively, that the sight of the sea, when it is right blue, is worth ten tons of *Campeche*."

"Is it possible!" exclaimed Anita, in a tone of profound astonishment, which melted gently into an accent of commiseration, as she added, "But the poor innocent lamb of a stranger don't know the value of *Campeche*."

Nevertheless, I hold stubbornly to my own estimate of the comparative value of my sea views, though it had not occurred to me to weigh it against logwood, before Juan hit on the happy idea.

Had I required additional stimulus to steady, unflagging exertion, I might have found it in the encouraging circumstances of my logwood cutting; but I did not need it. To work with an aim is to work with interest, and to work with interest is so healthful for mind and body, that there is no chance for miserable dyspepsia or for indolent repinings. My labors are acceptable, and my intervals of rest delightful.

I find it the most agreeable of relaxations to plan out my improvements, and to fit and adjust one occupation with another, so as to bring within the compass of each successive week the proper duties of its time and season. I want to feel and see that the labors of every month have been, to the best of my ability, such as most properly belong to that particular portion of the year.

My clearing and fencing are over for the present. My Home Field is in order for the plough, whenever the spring rains set in. When that time comes I shall be able to exchange my own labor, with my heavy American plough, for the use of oxen. Don Julio offers me, gratis, the use of two yoke of strong, though rather wild oxen, and a driver with them, in order to have them all instructed in that yet unknown mystery to Dominican agriculturists, the art of ploughing.

The season has not yet arrived for that; but I have plenty of occupation without it for the next six weeks in the care of my fruit-trees, and, *perhaps*, in putting up a poultry-yard.

I must think of *what* trees I require, of *where* I am to obtain them, *when* they should be planted, and, neither last nor least, *how* I am to place them to the best advantage, both with reference to their respective demands on soil, and their symmetrical relations with the situation of a future dwelling on my chosen site of Buena Vista.

There are many bearing fruit-trees on my homestead, eight or nine varieties at least; but there is a serious lack of sweet orange-trees. There are limes and sour oranges, plenty for my use, and always in bearing, it would seem; but no trees bearing the large, juicy sweet oranges, for which Santo Domingo has an old and well-deserved renown.

I want an orange grove for the enjoyment of its wholesome, delicious fruit, and for the preparation of that most delicate of tonics, "orange wine." I have tasted it at Don Julio's hospitable board, and am impatient to see it at my own.

I have a fair beginning at hand in a wild, chance-sown nursery of year old seedlings, which both Juan and Don Julio assure me will bear in three years, if left where they stand. But I have no idea of letting them stand, for they have nearly every one planted themselves in the wrong place. I must teach them how to shoot and where to grow, for I have my own plan as to what I shall do with them.

Early in January I noticed these clusters of young oranges struggling for life under a suffocating load of wild vines, along the line of the old hedge. I carefully relieved them at the time from their encroaching enemies, and partially trimmed off the crooked and superfluous shoots. Juan was eager to bring his *machete* to my aid, but his slashing activity was much too energetic for the health of my tender yearlings. I told him that I must reserve them for my own mornings' recreation until the rains came on, when I would be glad to have him help me to transplant such as I should select along the spring walk.

Juan heard the plan of transplanting with amazement. "Transplant these things, Señor!" he exclaimed; "why, these are nothing but sour oranges. Ah, yes, here are two—three—four sweet ones, but they are very well here. All the rest will give you fruit as sour as limes, only fit to make orangeade for sick people. *They* may live or die anywhere, as God pleases."

"But, Juan, I must place them where they will

have room to grow, and in time make a pleasant shade, to protect us from the sun and rain as we go to the spring and back. Besides that, I intend in due time that every one of these trees shall bear plenty of the finest sweet oranges, like those in your garden."

"How is it possible, Señor, to turn ugly sour oranges into large, beautiful sweet ones, like those Anita brings you?" queried Juan, somewhat doubtfully.

"Perfectly possible, Juan. I will engage to change the nature of their bearing so as to make every one of these wild, sour orange-trees yield none but the sweetest fruit—exactly like your own, in fact—provided you will give me some cuttings from the tree before your door."

"Oh, Señor, you know that the whole tree, body and branches, is at your service. But when will you perform the miracle?"

"About the first of March we will try to begin it, but in the mean time we have our February pruning to finish. Every thing in its season, Juan."

The last of our February work was the opening of a small trench in the winter garden to let in water from the spring. The dry weather tells more severely than I expected on my vegetables and garden relishes. The tomatoes hold up their heads, and are well set with young fruit as large as marbles, and the beans yield me a green mess every day for my dinner, but most of the other things seem to bear feebly. They are growing fairly in stem and leaf, but the fruit does not satisfy my expectations.

I have delved out with the pickaxe and hoe a foot-wide trench, which, opening its trunk at the margin of the spring, ramifies in crossing and expanding branches so as to conduct threads of water through most of the beds. It has cost me several days hard toil, with four half days of hired work from Juan, but it has secured the well-being of my plants, and I have a strong faith that the abundant and varied produce of this bit of ground will well repay the trouble.

I have worked and watched their progress with too much interest, not to be sensible of the fresh and improved appearance of my plants since I sent the trickling overplus of the spring meandering among them, and, for every hour I have given them, they will return me days and weeks of increased comfort and health. This much at least I have learned, and earned, in the first two months of working experience in my new country.

CHAPTER IV.

MARCH.

Fruits and flowers.—Charms of tropical life.—A visit from Juan's cousins.—What they wanted.—A strange "baptism."—Preparations for grafting—Startled by the appearance of a crowd around my tent.—The "convita."—My "neighbors and well-wishers."—Grafting performed in presence of a large company.—Pronounced a "miracle."—The great feast.—My address.—How responded to.—José Ravela.—We resolve to make a road to Palenque.—Don Julio's surprise.—He promises assistance.—The road finished.—Ignorance, not industry, debasing.

A PERPETUAL succession of fruits and flowers is one of the peculiar charms of tropical life, and March, like February, belongs emphatically to fruit culture. The pruning-knife and saw may be used moderately in January and freely in February, but March is the month for the final trimming and most reliable grafting of all kinds of fruit-trees, except those absolutely in the heart of their bearing season.

Juan had talked all through February of the grafting exploits we were to perform in March. Some of the neighbors had a dim idea of the process, but none had ever witnessed it, and there was quite a stir of expectation around and about me, though I was altogether unconscious of it until the day of action arrived.

On the last evening of February, I was bending over the closing notes of the month's summary, when the hum of voices outside of the tent aroused my attention. It was Juan, attended by a brace of cousins, who had come to ask formal permission to be present at "the *baptism* of my young orange-trees." For a moment, I was at a loss for the meaning of this odd phrase; but Juan explained it by reference to the sour orange-trees which I was to convert into bearers of sweet oranges of the first class, by some peculiar process which his friends were anxious to behold.

"Oh, certainly," said I. "Juan and his friends are heartily welcome to all I can show them. We will name next Monday morning for our grafting experiment. But I must first prepare my grafting salve, and, to make it properly, I must beg Anita to favor me with a lump of her nice beeswax."

"*En hora buena*," exclaimed Juan, joyously. "In a good hour. My lily of a wife"—Juan had the habit of calling his ebony spouse his "rose" and his "lily" when his spirits were elated—"my Anita said only to-day that she ought to bring you some new honey, and when the smoke is going, and my hands are among the hives, I will see that you have plenty of wax. Never fear for that, Señor."

"A piece the size of a hen's egg will be sufficient for all the trees I propose to graft. Don't trouble yourself or Anita to provide more than that."

"But does not the Señor want something from the apothecary at Bani for this famous salve?" inquired one of the cousins, in an anxious tone. "If he does, I will walk over there to-night, and bring it to him before noon to-morrow."

"No, thank you. Except the wax, I have all I require in that tin cup on the shelf. I take a bit of candle and as much rosin, or, as I have no rosin, as much tar as the tallow and wax together, and I have all I want. These three ingredients well mixed and melted, and spread on strips of old rags of any kind, is the whole story of this grafting salve. I hope you will all remember and practise it."

"*Wax* and *tar* and *tallow*," said Juan's other cousin, in a tone of surprise nearly allied to unbelief, "*nothing* but wax, tar, and tallow to baptize a sour orange into a sweet one! Why, Señor, that stuff is what we use to cure an ox or a burro when he gets a bad cut."

"Nothing else is needed, I assure you. Fruit-trees are as easily treated as oxen and donkeys. Only remember my directions, and practise carefully the proper method of uniting the young slips of sweet orange with the stems of the roughest and wildest nature, and you may have as many fruit-trees of the best quality as you wish, or have ground to plant in."

With this recommendation, which they promised not to forget, my visitors departed in high good humor, and left me to my solitary but never lonely repose. I am too full of occupation for lonesomeness

—which is the oppressing genius of men without an aim.

On the appointed day, not only Juan and *his* wife with his cousins and *their* wives, but at least a round dozen of their friends, male and female, were on the ground. After an early cup of coffee, I had gone over to Juan's cottage to cut scions from the superior fruit-tree at his door. When I returned I was a good deal startled at seeing a crowd gathered around my tent. I felt reassured, however, when Juan's cousin Anselmo detached himself from the group, and informed me that these were all my "neighbors and well-wishers, who had come to see—with my permission, and if I found nothing improper in their presence—how I performed the miracle of changing the nature of a tree from bad to good."

Anselmo had the idea rooted in his mind that there was some occult, though benign, charm in the proposed operation. In his simple fancy, it had a kind of assimilation to the sacred rite which hallows the infant brow, and brings it within the fold of Christianity.

There was not the remotest tinge of irreverence in their unsophisticated hearts, and I felt that the shortest way of explaining the simple and material nature of the change to be wrought in the fruits yet to be borne by these hardy stocks, would be to show the exact character of the operation.

With a few brief words of welcome, I invited them to the scene of business. They thanked me with impressive solemnity, and moved in mass to the point indicated, where they took their assigned places with the grave decorum of a Committee of Observation, duly authorized to carefully watch and exactly report every step of the important process.

I could hardly repress a smile as Juan stepped about, his countenance charged with the deepest expression of responsibility, ranging his men in a standing semicircle on one side, and seating the women under Anita's captainship on the grass, opposite their liege lords, but a little farther removed from the centre of operations.

I asked two of them to come forward and notice the young trees before I beheaded them; that they might see for themselves that they were then but saplings of the common sour orange, although they were never to be permitted to bear other than large, sweet fruit, exactly like that of their neighbor Juan's, which, be it said, is the admiration of all that circle.

"There are three limes here besides the seventeen oranges," observed Juan sedately, not for *my* benefit —for we had counted them half a dozen times over— but for a little stage effect on his own account.

"I think we will make sweet oranges of the limes also, while we are about it, Juan." A suppressed murmur of amazed delight was the only reply, as I advanced to open the play.

The salve and bandages were ready, as well as the scions, which, as I have already noted, Juan and I had cut early in the morning. As I successively headed down and cleft the stem of each young tree, Juan, previously instructed in his part, with two smooth strokes of his knife, cut the scion butt into a long, true wedge, and handed it to me to insert in the stock. The instant my knife parted the cleft,

Anita, and an aide-de-camp cousin, honored for the day with the charge of the twine, delivered the bandage, to be wound well and firmly over the union of scion and stock, and assisted in tying it all in place. In this order we went from tree to tree, till every one had received the crowning graft, and then for the first moment did the anxious company unbend from its rigid attitude of attention, and break forth into the warmest expressions of applause.

More numerous and distinguished spectators may have cheered the experimental labors of a Franklin, while seducing the lightning from its wild path in the heavens, or a Jenner, while spreading the mild glories of vaccination, but neither of them ever had an audience more trustful and appreciative, than the breathless circle whose eyes followed with reverential faith every motion of the two jack-knives and of the ancient tin cup, while employed in doing the honors of that grafting day.

I have no doubt that nearly every man then present will try his hand at grafting fruit-trees in some fashion, and without much regard to time and season, but I shall feel well satisfied if any one of them really succeeds.

I was careful to explain to them that the most suitable time is towards the close of the dry season, when the sap is concentrated, and disposed to rush into vigorous circulation with the early rains; but few of that class will remember it. Yet it will be well for new-comers in this sunny and abounding land to give some heed to these lessons.

Trees may be safely relieved of that luxuriant surplusage of branches, so noticeable in most tropical countries, at almost any season of the year; but the time for regular and complete pruning is between December and May, when the circulation is languid, and nature declines exhausting her powers in impetuous efforts to sprout new shoots where the old ones are lopped.

Men of practical experience have assured me that a judicious trimming in January or February gave an advantage equal to a year's growth in oranges, mango, mamey, and other young fruit-trees,—most of them being larger, more beautiful, and bearing better at three years, than others in the same grounds, which were left to themselves, at four, and even five years from the seed.

There is generally in the Antilles a period of "forty dry days," some time between the first of February and the last of March, and this is the chosen period for pruning and grafting.

My grafting for the current year was begun, and in all probability was finished, on the memorable first Monday of March, which I am now chronicling at this egotistical length. In truth, my kind neighbors made it such a pleasant day that I love to dwell on it.

It was near eleven when the last crowning scion received the final knot on its bandage, and I was not sorry to be done with it, and turn to the cool shade of my embowered tent for an hour's repose.

As I drew back the curtain to enter, I discovered Anita and her little daughter Teresa buzzing about like two distracted bees, in the vain endeavor to dispose in neat order a dozen independent heaps of fruits and vegetables, scattered on the floor, on the table, on the boxes that do duty for sofas and chairs, on every thing, in brief, and in every corner that would hold them.

"What in the name of wonder is all this, Anita?"

"Oh, nothing, Señor. The '*convita*' (the party of invited guests) knew the Señor was a stranger in our country, and each of them brought a yam, or some cassava, or a handful of potatoes, or any *nadita* (little nothing) from their own grounds, so as not to give the Señor the least trouble about their breakfast."

"Then we are to give all these people a regular breakfast?" I demanded in consternation, as my scant store of camp cups and plates, not to mention wherewith to fill them, flashed across my mind.

"Don't be concerned, Señor," said Anita, with the triumphant composure of an able general, serenely conscious that his well-planned arrangements have secured victory to his banners. "Juan and I have prepared every thing."

"Is this splendid breakfast to be laid out here, Anita?" I inquired, in helpless despair, glancing round at the narrow limits of the tent.

"God forbid, Señor," said the woman, hastily. "We know better than to take such a liberty with the Señor's private apartment."

'Where then is the affair to come off?" I asked, greatly relieved by this declaration.

"I will show the Señor, if he will please to walk this way," she answered, radiant with the feminine delight of having managed a success.

I followed her docilely to the door of the old cabin. This had been cleared and repaired, to serve as a kitchen and store-room; and what with barrels, cart, plough, etc., it was reasonably full of a poor farmer's working gear; but while I was busy in the early morning, getting my scions and attending to the minutiæ of the grafting preparations, two of Anita's confidential friends had quietly slipped into possession.

I will not attempt to describe the process by which three barrels and a couple of planks were converted into a table; the plough and "cultivator" made the ornamental supports of a rustic sofa; while the cart and wheelbarrow loomed into the dignity of sideboards. Enough to say that those who planned the feast and shared in it, found it to their perfect satisfaction.

The company were not present when I went to survey the hall of entertainment; Juan had considerately led them off to the site of Buena Vista, to show them how thrifty and symmetrical those trees were growing which we had trimmed in January. When they returned it was about noon, and the breakfast was ready for them.

As to the feast, I can only chronicle that an enormous baked fish came from I know not where, and a vast platter of stewed kid, formidable to the eye, but of fragrant odor, was rushing in on the head of a tattered youngster from other unknown regions. These, with a Spanish "*san coche*" composed of pig, pigeon, and plantain—excuse the alliteration—were the staple dishes. An unlimited supply of corn-cakes and warm vegetables was kept up by an old crone in charge of three or four fires back of the cabin, and whatever my biscuit barrel and a smaller one—whose contents shall be nameless—could do in the way of helping out this wildwood cheer, was frankly contributed.

My own simple noon meal was served to me apart in my tent, but when that and theirs were well over, I went to the cabin and circulated a bundle of native cigars among my native guests. Not being compelled to smoke them myself, I was quite regardless of the expense, which, for the benefit of future immigrants, who should *always* have some on hand to offer to country visitors, I will mention, is something less than a cent each.

After eating, drinking, lounging, and smoking until about two, the whole party, headed by Juan, filed up before the tent, to offer their aid for the afternoon in completing my fence. That was a piece of business at which so many hands could not be employed to advantage, and I proposed, in its stead, to name something which I said ought to interest all the neighbors.

A quiet little fellow, named José Ravela, promptly answered, in the name of his companions, that they had come to offer me their services in whatever way would be most acceptable, and I had only to signify my wishes.

I pointed out, in a few words, that the neighborhood was utterly destitute of a cart road to the port, though it was but a mile distant from their centre of settlement at the edge of the prairie.

"Does Señor Vecino (Señor neighbor) say we ought to make this road?" asked José, evidently taken by surprise.

"Yes," I boldly replied, "and we ought to make it now while the season favors us. If we unite our efforts for one day in a week, we can open for ourselves a fine, firm, straight road in a couple of months. It will harden and improve while our crops are growing, and when they are gathered we can take them to Palenque in carts, at half the expense and trouble it now costs to carry them as you do, on the backs of mules and donkeys."

"Enough. We are all ready to follow you in the work," was the cordial response of the most influential voices present.

This road had occupied my thoughts for some

time, and I had carefully examined the lay of the land. In effect, the line of the road was so easy and obvious, that I had in a measure traced it out in advance. This volunteer force enabled me to begin it well, and, once begun, I could foresee a way to have it completed.

The great coast highway from Santo Domingo to Azua skirts our savanna for several miles, leaving a belt of woodland, between it and the sea, but sparsely dotted with small cleared fields. Mine lay about midway between the prairie edge and the Bay of Palenque, but I had no more interest than the poorest of my farming neighbors in opening this cross road from the highway along the savanna to our common seaport at Palenque, and all of us together scarcely as much as any one of the large landowners like Don Julio Perez, who were weekly shipping their sugar and fine woods from this point.

Armed with axe and machete, my neighbors and I lost no time in commencing the work at the nearest point, according to my plan; and, taking the direction of Palenque, we cut away with such energy, that by sunset we had opened a long vista between the walls of verdure on either hand, to the unbounded satisfaction of the company. There were no large trees to dispose of, and the nature of the ground is extremely favorable; so our progress was rapid, and our industry told well to the eyes and hearts of the laborers.

The idea of a road of "our own," where it was so much needed and so easily made, captivated all, and before we dispersed it was unanimously agreed that the neighbors should again unite their forces and continue the work for three successive Saturdays at least.

On this I told the company that I felt that we had earned the right to call on Don Julio Perez and the large proprietors, who used Palenque as the shipping port for their rice, sugar, and precious woods, to do their proportion towards opening a road so useful to their leading objects of business. My hearers were perfectly enchanted with the brilliant audacity of an appeal to the rich proprietors, and pledged themselves over and over again, with great heartiness, to undertake with me the half of the road on our prairie side, if Don Julio would engage for himself and friends to make the portion that traversed their own wild lands around Palenque.

When I broached the matter to him I fancied that Don Julio was slightly astonished at the bold urgency of a poor stranger, but I insisted upon his attention to its bearings on his own interests, and won from him a promise that he and his friends would do their part, after *I* and *my* humble friends (who were so much less able, and so much less to be profited by it) had fulfilled our proportion of the undertaking.

Resolved not to spare my own full share of effort, I spent most of the week in chopping up and removing to one side of the lane the brush which remained in the way. My new fence was lined with it, and to this Juan and I put the finishing bars and stakes as we went along. It was done on Thursday, and my field was now not only completely enclosed, but every tree in it carefully trimmed of dead and superfluous limbs. All of Friday was given to marking out the work for my neighbors, when they should collect in force for road-making the next day.

They were true to their word, and the day's work told wonderfully. The first twenty yards were close chapparal, but beyond that stretched a long grassy strip of plain ground, which gave us, ready made, near three hundred yards of excellent road from nature's own hand. Farther on, our lane cut through the border of an abandoned field, leaving on either hand just enough young trees to ensure a charming shade.

Placing Juan with two assistants at one end of this troublesome patch of chapparal, and José Ravela on the opposite side, I directed them to cut towards each other until they met, while I crossed the open glade with the main force and continued the lane onward. By so doing the two sections laid off for the forenoon were both well opened at half-past eleven, when we called a rest.

We had our luncheon on another small open glade, at the termination of the second section of the morning's work. From thence we looked back with delight, through a beautiful straight lane, to the point of commencement.

The afternoon's work did not show so well; for after passing the old field, and the little glade beyond it where the former cultivator once had his cottage and door-yard, we entered the real forest. But this was the domain of Don Julio, and, in strict justice, to him rather than to us belonged the charge of the road hence to the sea. Our remaining work lay at the other end of the line, towards the prairie, and was to be resumed at our first starting-point and carried out to where it would strike, nearly at right angles, the royal highway. Still we dented our lane a few rods into the forest border, so as to connect it with a beaten horse-path, leading down to the port and fishing-grounds of Palenque; and we worked zealously to effect this before we separated.

The axe was still ringing, and the machete merrily plying among the falling limbs, when Don Julio rode in among us from the winding Palenque path. He trampled through and over the last felled branches, and reined up at the head of the long line of light opened by our lane, with a strong exclamation of delighted surprise. That one long, earnest gaze through the clear vista carried a more direct conviction to his heart than a thousand arguments. In showing him what we *had* done, it told him what he *ought* to do. When he spoke it was to the purpose.

"This road is exactly what we want, my friends," he said, warmly :—" what every man with a ceroon of sugar or a stick of timber has suffered for these thirty years, and it shall be finished forthwith."

This announcement was received with enthusiasm, and the spirit of mutual helpfulness which took form that evening has been in active operation the whole month, and with the month the road has been completed.

March has been what it should be, by natural laws, —a season of fruit-grafting and road-making. The last Sunday of the month, Don Julio sent a horse for me to join him and a party of his friends in a ride to the peerless bathing-coves of Palenque, through our new and straight road, and through it back again to a supper at his house.

I return from it to close my record for the month, and to add that the fact of my working among workingmen for my daily bread has not unfitted me, either in my own estimation, nor, so far as I can see, in the estimation of Don Julio's aristocratic circle, for the free interchange of useful plans and ideas, if I happen to possess any, with these privileged "exempts" from manual toil. Remember, honest fellow-toiler, *it is ignorance, not industry, that dwarfs and debases those men without manhood who would rather beg than work.*

CHAPTER V.

APRIL.

Ploughing-match at Don Julio's.—Stupid native.—Unruly oxen.—An unlooked-for assistant.—Don Delfino de Castro.—Achieve a great victory.—Compliments and congratulations.—Return to Buena Vista.—Important changes.—An "Eden of tranquillity."—A guest for the night.—He proposes to remain longer.—Camp cooking and coffee-making.—Compact with Don Delfino.—What we do together.—His man Isidro.—Beautiful appearance of my orange avenue.—Plentiful showers.—Fragrant blossoms.—Crowning triumph of my garden.

FRAGRANT April has come and gone. Balmy and flower-laden is April everywhere, but eminently fragrant and blossoming here, where fruits and flowers crown every month of the year with garlands of beauty. Strictly speaking, the "wet season" commences in May, but there are few years in which the frequent and refreshing showers of April will not justify early planting, particularly of corn, potatoes, and beans, *all of them most excellent and paying crops in the West Indies.* It is always within the compass of the poorest man, if he is willing to work, to produce these crops in sufficient abundance for the comfortable support of a plain farmer's family.

Juan, who has stood by me so faithfully in my clearing, fencing, road-making, and fruit culture, is now busy in getting his own crop in the ground, and can only work for me two or three forenoons in the week. I had arranged my plans to meet this limited amount of help, when a timely accession of aid and encouragement burst in from a most unexpected quarter.

Don Julio had offered to lend me a yoke of oxen to break up my land, and I had proffered in return the use of my plough to turn up an old field adjoining his house, which he desired to plant with coffee. I had no will to trust my heavy plough to his ignorant field-hands and ill-trained oxen, and therefore proposed to do the work myself at a specified time.

We had several falls of rain in the first two weeks of April; and a succession of three smart showers within the space of seven days is warrant enough for any farmer to begin his planting in Santo Domingo. It had rained nearly the whole afternoon and night of Saturday, and when the plough and I made our appearance at Don Julio's, early on Monday, we found not only the ground in a splendid condition to do us credit, but also a goodly company assembled to award us all the honor plough and I could possibly win by our best efforts.

The oxen were led out, the plough attached, and the first furrow laid off with great éclat, but on turning the second, the oxen—probably discovering that there was something unusual and un-Dominican in these proceedings—suddenly became obstinate and unruly.

The man who worked them was rather more stupid and unmanageable than the oxen, and for a moment we had an awkward "balk" in the ploughing. A Señor Delfino de Castro, who had come over from his farm on the San Cristoval road—a man endowed with that most uncommon gift among the Dominicans, the right manly use of his hands—promptly stepped to the rescue. Dismissing the confused and clamorous negro driver, Don Delfino took the guidance of the half-wild oxen, while I held the plough. The piece laid off for the first day contained twelve tascas—that is to say, the full allotment of twelve days' work for an able-bodied man to cut up with the hoe—and, as I proved it afterwards, not far from half an acre.

As the deep true furrows were run, and line after line of clean dark loam lay upturned to the fertilizing sun and showers, and to such purpose as no man present except myself had ever seen the soil cut and stirred before, the first deep silence of watchful doubt turned into murmurs of pleased surprise. When the last ribbon of green was turned under and disappeared before the cleaving ploughshare, the whole company gathered round Delfino and myself, to overpower us with compliments and congratulations.

How strongly did I realize that there is a true dignity in labor when it is useful and well performed, and when the laborer does not disgrace himself and his calling by being ashamed of it. This circle of wealthy non-workers were at least competent to balance the results of that forenoon with the plough against the shallow, uncertain work of twelve men with the heavy native hoe, and estimate its value. It was even more than so much human labor saved, for in the effective preparation of the soil we had done the work of twenty men, as the Dominicans manage it.

Not one of that circle, except Delfino, had the force, moral, mental, or physical, to do the same, but not the less did they, one and all, treat us—the hard-handed victors of toil—as the especial and honored guests of the noble entertainment which Don Julio had ordered for the celebration of what he was pleased to call the "introduction of Prince Plough to his agricultural subjects in his future realm of Santo Domingo."

It was a brilliant evening for me. The remarks of those educated and high-bred gentlemen were of absorbing interest, and promise an abiding utility in my guidance. I enjoyed much, and learned more, in the social flow of Dominican thoughts, habits, and experiences, and I left the charming circle with regret.

Don Julio urged me to remain for the night, but I had work laid out at home which I could not afford to neglect; but, that done, I promised to return and finish ploughing the field which we had commenced with so much honor.

The next morning but one found me at his place bright and early, and the day after also; which finished the field, and my engagement, and left me free to plough and plant for myself, with the use of a strong pair of oxen as long as I required.

Yet this interval of three days had wrought some changes of no mean importance to my plan of life. They originated on the memorable evening of the plough festival, which I had passed so agreeably in the social circle of Don Julio and his intimates, but which I was forced to leave rather early, to be home in reasonable season, and ready to attend betimes to some work set apart for the morrow.

On leaving, Don Delfino said he should bear me company a part of the way, and we started together.

The night was soft as June, the road open and level all the way—thanks to our exertions in cutting a straight lane through the timber—and the conversation so interesting that Delfino made no motion of turning back until we stood side by side before my tent, looking round at the beautiful effect of the star-light on the open space, belted in by a dark wall of woodlands, and picturesquely dotted by the groups of fruit-trees rescued from the wilderness.

"What an Eden of tranquillity!" said Delfino. "It disinclines me to return to Don Julio's to-night."

"I have a spare hammock, Don Delfino, and this tent and cot are altogether at your service, if you will favor me with your company."

"*Mil gracias*,—a thousand thanks—but I will not consent to rob you of your house. I am an old campaigner, and want nothing better than the hammock. In a word, it shall be that and nothing else, or I go back to Don Julio's. Which say you?"

"Oh, the hammock, by all means, since you leave me no choice, and I will sling it at once," I answered, moving into the tent to strike a light and begin operations.

"First tell me what this is," interrupted Delfino,

taking the direction of the old cabin, which is now completely embowered in a palisade of Lima beans in full bearing.

"That is my workshop, tool-house, and kitchen, Don Delfino. Here, in this rustic porch of my own construction, my meals are cooked. You can see my calabash bowls and cocoa-nut cups on that shelf. This is my dining-table, made out of the smallest of the two packing-boxes in which I brought my effects; the largest supplied me that cupboard beside the door."

"You are an independent hermit, *amigo mio*," said Delfino, gayly, "and I am glad to see you light up the interior of this sanctum, that I may study it the more closely."

I had touched a match to a candle while he was speaking, and held it up to give him the view he desired.

"What can this fantastic little plough do?" He had glanced into every corner with the restless curiosity of a school-boy let loose in a lumber-room, and now brought out a small patent "cultivator," with as much glee as the same school-boy might feel on the discovery of a three-wheeled cart in some dark recess.

"That fantastic little plough, as you call it, Don Delfino, is intended to cut down the weeds in planted fields, is made very light, though strong, to be drawn by a small donkey. The donkey is the cheapest animal-power in this country, and therefore the most suitable for a poor beginner like me."

"This is something really new," said Delfino, examining it with attention, "and almost as important as the plough. When do you expect to use the little beauty?"

"To-morrow morning," I replied. "These late showers have brought out a rank crop of weeds in what I call my winter garden. They must be cut down before I begin any new work, or even finish Don Julio's ploughing."

"To-morrow morning," exclaimed Delfino. "To-morrow morning. Then I shall see the performance. Let me be your *burroquero*—your donkey-driver?" I could not but smile at Delfino's enthusiasm, but I told him that one man, or, for that matter, a boy of twelve years, would be quite sufficient for the management of both the donkey and the weeder.

"Nevertheless I shall ask your permission to learn the use of this gem of an earth-cutter to-morrow," said Delfino. "And like the knight of old, on the vigil of his initiation, I shall sleep by my weapons," he added, seizing upon the hammock, which just then caught his eye suspended from the rafters.

"But the tent is much more cool and pleasant," I remonstrated, "and it would pain me to have you lodged midst this chaos of farming utensils."

"I have made a vow to sleep here this night," replied the self-willed Delfino, tightening the hammock cords as he spoke. "Not only this night, but, if God pleases, and you do not object, *amigo mio*, many other nights. I intend to enlist under the flag of Prince Plough and General Weeder, if you will consent to be my captain."

"I shall be proud of my soldier," I answered, catching the light, laughing spirit of my self-elected guest and pupil. "But you will please to remember that obedience is a primary military duty, and I, in virtue of my captainship, insist on your instantly taking up your quarters in the tent."

"Pardon me, captain," replied Delfino, throwing himself into the hammock. "But it is a condition precedent to enlistment, that no soldier can possibly be ordered to commit such a scandalous breach of military propriety as to usurp his officer's personal quarters. Such an impossibility is out of the sphere of discussion."

Finding Delfino immovable in his resolutions, I left him in possession of the cabin and retired to my tent for the night. When I awoke in the morning it was already sunrise, and I started up in haste, to prepare for my guest the early cup of coffee with which the Dominicans begin the day. As I turned the corner of the cabin to enter the arbor kitchen, I beheld Delfino in high stir among the cups and coffee, by the lighted fire. I well-nigh forgot the courtesy of a morning salutation in my astonishment at the grave intentness of his preoccupation.

"Do you propose studying camp cookery as well

as Yankee farming under my direction, Don Delfino?" I inquired as I joined him.

"Drop all titles, and call me Delfino simply and frankly, like a true friend and worthy instructor. Learn camp cookery of you, my captain? No, it is I who will have to teach you that delicate art. Here, for example, I offer you a cup of coffee worthy the palate of a professor of agriculture."

"But really, Don Delfino"—I began, but I was cut short with—"Really, my Captain, you should not descend to these altercations with Delfino the pupil, much less with Delfino the cook. Sip your coffee in peace, and leave the culinary department to me."

The coffee was disposed of, and the "weeder" brought forth for duty without waste of time, for the cool morning hours are precious in this climate. The donkey was a rough and ragged concern of Juan's, but, like all his race, patient and steady.

When he was fairly started, Delfino would hear of nothing but taking the entire charge of weeding the plat. "Burro is in my line," said he. "We are brother Dominicans and perfectly understand each other;" and away he went, driving the animal through the close lines of beans, corn, ocra, and young tomatoes, with much more expertness than I had yet acquired in managing the beast.

We had to contrive a muzzle to prevent his nipping the tender plants right and left, but we finally cured him of the trick, when Burro became—as he did two weeks later—my own property.

The morning wore on, but Delfino, so far from being daunted by the heat and grime of this unusual labor, was enchanted with his success. The ease and perfection with which the light cultivator shears off the weeds, and throws the loosened earth about the roots of the plants, delighted him beyond measure. He entreated me to leave him alone to finish the last remaining section of my March planting, while I went along with the hoe among the borders of ginger and arrowroot, edging the cross path of the winter garden.

As Delfino really left me no option on that point, I did as he wished.

Ginger and arrowroot resemble each other in their long, bright, green leaves, somewhat like those of the common garden lily, and besides the value of their productive roots, they form a beautiful border to walks and vegetable plats. I had collected the bulbs from the grounds of my neighbors, but mainly from Don Julio's garden, and the neat effect of these miniature hedges, defining the pathways to the spring and through the garden, had elicited flattering comments from Delfino.

I did not complete my task until the sun rode almost noon high, but Delfino had already run the "weeder" through every row of corn and vegetables open to it, and was repeating the operation quite needlessly, here and there, when I came to take Burro out of harness.

Juan had brought over the donkey very early, by appointment, and I took occasion to send a private hint to Anita that her aid would be welcome in providing a dinner for my visitor. I did not, therefore, feel so much surprise as Delfino manifested, on finding a warm and not unpalatable meal ready for us when we returned to the cabin arbor to wash off the dust of the morning's toil.

We were lounging away the usual after-dinner hour of rest, chatting of books, politics, and farming in quiet ease, Delfino always talking as if it was perfectly understood that I was to teach him all I knew myself respecting the most improved implements of husbandry, when he suddenly renewed his proposal "to commence his agricultural studies practically and immediately."

"You do not think I am serious when I assure you that I am anxious to live here and work for you a month or two," said he, abruptly, dashing away his cigar, and turning around with an air of almost defiant determination, that startled me into sober attention.

"You live here in this wild way, Don Delfino? A gentleman of your habits and position undertake to work for me? You must be dreaming—or I am," I exclaimed.

"Peter of Russia lived no better and worked as hard among the shipwrights of Holland, when he went to learn how to create a navy. He was an Emperor, and had the power to build ships without working on them himself, but I am only a plain Dominican planter, and there is no way for me to acquire the capacity to create such a place as I want, and such as I mean to possess, unless I put my own eyes and hands to the work."

"But my arrangements are so miserably inadequate," I continued, glancing at the obvious poverty of my domestic surroundings.

"Never fear for that," answered Delfino, gayly; "what we cannot amend we will endure. Let us fancy ourselves travellers exploring a newly-discovered country. We will rejoice together over the difficulties we conquer and the novelties we win, instead of repining for what we have voluntarily left behind."

"Be it as you will," I said at last, finding argument useless; "but let me warn you," I added, seriously, "that mine is a workingman's life in hard earnest. I am a poor man struggling to make a home, and my steady toil and coarse fare cannot suit one of your habits."

"Try me," replied Delfino, laughing. "You have no right to set me down as an idle gourmand, incapable of useful efforts, until you have measured me fairly. But here comes one of our friend Julio's servants, to remind us that we sup with him this evening."

Delfino replied to the message for both of us, but he would not start for Don Julio's until after he had made the round of my fruit-trees in the afternoon. The pulpy custard apple, the delicate caimeto, and the refreshing soursop, were full of ripe, delicious fruit. These were the old trees which I had relieved of dead limbs and the suffocating thicket of January, and they now loom up grandly on the left side of the Buena Vista Mound.

"That clump of lofty and spreading trees would be an ornament to the finest grounds in America," I observed to Delfino; "such groups are very common here; yet few Dominicans seem to appreciate their beauty, or value the luxury of a succession of choice fruits the whole year through."

"It is human nature to undervalue blessings so

freely bestowed," said Delfino: "but what is all this? Have you a hospital of maimed and bandaged trees?"

He had stopped to examine my grafted orange-trees. I explained the process, of which he had read something, but now saw for the first time in operation. The grafts were putting forth their fresh crowns, and all were doing well.

"You will have abundance of oranges in two or three years," said Delfino, at the close of my explanations, "but are not these trees too close together?"

"I hope to transplant them, about the close of this month, in a double line along the walk I am laying off from the spring to Buena Vista—the site, if God prospers the wish, of my future dwelling."

"I too will plant an orange avenue this very year," said Delfino, as we walked back to the house. "It must wait, however, till our corn-fields are planted, for we cannot be sure of two full crops before December, if the April planting is not a foot high the first morning in May."

We went together to sup and sleep at Don Julio's, and to talk over with him Delfino's project of working awhile with me at Buena Vista. Don Julio enjoyed the idea exceedingly, and pointed out means for several minor accommodations, which we acted upon at once.

Anita, for example, was engaged as a sort of day housekeeper, and Delfino observed that he had an active, intelligent young man named Isidro on his place, who should be sent down immediately, with a stout horse for the single plough, to learn the art of ploughing in company with his master.

All this was speedily settled upon, and after a flying visit home Delfino himself joined us in two days after, and with this force the farming business went on rapidly. The heavy ox plough went through all its share of the work in ten days. Delfino and I ploughed in the forenoon, and Isidro took his turn in the afternoon.

The "brush harrow" which I improvised, in default of the legitimate article, amused Delfino hugely. It would have been a sight to a gentleman farmer of the United States to see him managing his horse with this immense bundle of brush on one side of the ploughed ground, while I followed him with the donkey, "marking" off the corn-rows. This, and planting the corn, was our afternoon's work when it did not rain, and in three days after Don Julio's oxen were sent home my ground was all seeded in. Juan and Anita volunteered their aid—she in dropping and he in covering the corn, as fast as Delfino harrowed and I marked off the ground. So many hands made speedy work, and Delfino never flagged until the ploughing and planting were fully and thoroughly finished.

My crop is now well above ground. Don Delfino and his man Isidro left me to return home this morning,—I am writing these last lines on May-day eve,—and with them went my heavy plough, on a six weeks' loan.

On average returns my corn, which in this climate ought to be in market in September, will pay for clearing and planting twenty acres more by October. Meanwhile, I have an abundant supply of vegetables for my own use, and also to exchange with my neighbors for the eggs, poultry, honey, and cassava bread which they bring to me almost every evening. *They* lost the dry season, because they scorned the labor of making and tending seedling beds. The care of a garden through the dry months they thought an unprofitable toil, yet they do not scruple to barter with me for my overplus of products, in return for many little comforts which I want of them, on what is to me a most convenient and profitable system of exchange.

By the middle of April, I had almost every variety of vegetables that is to be found in the New York markets in June; and therefore it is I wish to note, that whoever is willing to devote to it a few days' labor, may keep up a constant supply the whole year in this favored climate.

Four months have fled by, like a pleasant though busy dream, since I laid myself down to my first night's repose in my "homestead." The Giver of all good gifts has crowned my poor efforts with His tender mercies, and as I look up from these pages to glance through the arcade of fruit-yielding trees, and onward to the gentle hill-side, now green with springing corn, and beautiful in the promise of future abundance, I feel a fervent and grateful trust—far, far too deep for my weak powers of utterance—that He will never forsake the humble and trustful laborer in this fair field of His creation.

CHAPTER VI.

MAY.

Fresh encouragemont.—Site for a new house.—The Mango Avenue.—A "trifling incident."—A rustic gate.—A shipwrecked sailor.—What in search of.—Visit from Captain Ramirez of the "Alice."—Satisfactory solution of a puzzling question.—A market for my vegetables.—Don Julio.—Ambitious projects.—Picturesque scenes.—Twenty-two kinds of fruits on my homestead.—An alluring picture.—An important addition to my revenue.—I hire two native woodmen.—The "New Field."—Grateful acknowledgments.

THE labors of the preceding months begin to speak encouragingly to the eye and the heart. My crop is waving greenly around me; I rest securely in the trustworthiness of my fences, and my fruit-trees are thriving to my entire satisfaction. From May to October, the season of almost daily rains, is the proper time for transplanting fruit-trees and shrubbery. During five months, when all planting is intermitted throughout the United States, the farmer in the tropics may keep on the whole period, putting in corn, cotton, sugar, and other crops, perfectly certain that they will all ripen to advantage in the last fall and first winter months, and that he will be sure to have delightful weather through most of January, and all of February and March, to gather in his successive harvests, and send them to market.

I have so much work before me which I must conquer single-handed—or be conquered by it—that I could scarcely hope to give more than eight or ten days of May to my favorite project, which is to lay out my grounds, and plant a large assortment of fruits early in the season.

I was anxious, also, about the means of clearing, fencing, and planting the southern portion of my homestead; not only because it is the richest and most level ground, and its profits needful to my support, but because opening it up would widen my sea prospect, let in more of the sea-breeze, and improve the health of the place, if it has any defects in that way. There are about twenty acres in this tract and much of it heavily timbered, so it was no light task for me to undertake with the scattering half day's help I might receive from Juan. Yet without breaking over one of my strictest self-imposed rules and running into the slavery of debt I saw no other way before me.

While meditating on this, I did not slacken my efforts to forward the work in hand, and went on preparing the ground for setting out long avenues of fruit-trees, for the comfort and adornment of my future house. The house itself is far in the future, years perhaps, but meantime, the site being chosen, and its frontage, if not its dimensions, well settled in mind, every tree and shrub can be placed in accordance with this centre and pivot of the general plan. The trees may be growing up, during this interval into shady avenues, and the shrubs may go on maturing in order and beauty, so that if there does come to me a day in which I can sit down to rest under my own commodious roof, all these surroundings will have ripened into a happy fitness, and make a complete and harmonious whole.

The "New Road" we had cut to bring Port Palenque into connection with the great coast highway, and the hamlets of Savanna Grande limits my land on that side, and naturally constitutes the base line of my programme of improvements. My hoped for dwelling—the darling air-castle of my secret thoughts—must outlet upon this road, and it must also face the sea breeze.

This establishes my points of departure for every line of tree planting and field fencing.

I am more than contented with the building site accorded to me. Buena Vista, crowning an airy eminence, with its pure, unfailing spring at no unreasonable distance, is far enough retired from the road to insure tranquillity, but not too far for convenient access. Here then I find my natural centre of operations and proper place of beginning.

I opened a clear lane, thirty feet wide, from the house site to the road, and there I constructed a rude gate. Patiently, painfully, steadily, I labored five days on that strip of ground; clearing out the smaller stumps and reducing the larger ones to the level of the ground, until the grade was complete and every serious obstacle removed. Along the road and running off in a line, on each side of the gate, I transplanted three almond-trees, selected from a cluster which I had stumbled upon in our clearings and preserved for this purpose.

The *almendra*, or wild almond, is a superb tree, of very rapid growth, and in three or four years a row of half a dozen on the line of the road will form a really ornamental shade to the homestead entrance.

From the gate up to the front of the house site, I planted a double line of *mangoes*, twenty feet apart, seven each side of the avenue. The oriental mango is a magnificent shade tree—to my mind it has no peer North or South—never changing, winter or summer, the deep-toned richness of its dense foliage, always yielding a peculiarly grateful shade, and rarely failing to give an abundance of delicious fruit in May and June, for it is a most generous bearer. From these fourteen mangoes I may—if alive and here—confidently hope to gather fruit in three years, when they will probably be something like twenty feet high. They are now only about twenty inches above ground, but they are sturdy growers. Don Julio has a pair of mangoes of which four years ago this month he put the seed in the ground, after eating the fruit at dinner. They are now loaded with golden fruit, and very nearly if not quite twenty feet high. From them I took the hint of my "mango avenue," and from his garden I also transplanted my young trees.

The preparation of the ground and the planting of thirty-six trees which I had collected here and there amongst my neighbors, ran away with the first week of May.

After the day's work was over, I would use the evening to forage the neighborhood for every variety of fruit-tree and ornamental shrub I could muster. My chief object was to secure a succession of at least three varieties of fruit—fresh and good for my own trees—for every week of the year. Another, though of course secondary, design was to dot the circular crest of Buena Vista with a line of flowering shrubs; not high enough to exclude the sea view, but sufficiently so to define the circuit of the house-grounds, while it regaled the senses with the beauty and fragrance of ever renewed blossoms.

A trifling incident stimulated me into a settled plan, and a persevering course of effort, to obtain a handsome array of ornamental plants, by teaching me the facility with which it could be accomplished.

The first Sabbath I awoke in this new home of mine I caught with the rising dew the sweet odor of roses. On looking around I discovered, almost under the eaves of the old cabin, a bush of deep crimson roses, crushed nearly out of sight by the entangling vines of a passion flower. I tore the vines apart and the next morning I cut some forked stakes and cross rods to frame a rustic trellis for the passion flower. The vine bears generously and its thick foliage screens, as I am now writing, the roost of a pair of fine guinea fowls.* The rose was left to grow in grace and bloom in luxuriant freedom by its side.

This was early in January, and now, at the close of May, my hardy rose is still crowned with flowers. How long it will continue in bearing I cannot say, but for the past five months it certainly has never been more than three days at a time without blossoms. This country is so kindly and fertile in vines and shrubbery that any man who will give a few hours work in these pleasant May mornings, for planting, and an occasional half hour through the summer for training and pruning the over luxuriance of stem and sprout, may convert the roughest cabin into a bower of beauty.

The God-given luxuries of fruits and flowers are almost as free as air on the Dominican soil, and he is an ingrate who declines the use of the beneficent gifts. The poorer the homestead, the more need of these softening adornments. They cost nothing but the trouble of planting them in proper mode and season, wherever you wish to have them. I had many more offered to me than I have space and leisure to do justice to, in return for the little gifts of early vegetables, which the moist soil of my winter garden enables me to distribute among my neighbors in all April.

But I must leave my ornamentals and return to the " utilities."

In clearing off the logwood thicket on the southern brow of Buena Vista, there remained a mass of small stuff, whose innumerable stumps, though quick to decay, would forbid the use of the plough the first season. Not to entirely lose the use of the ground, I planted it with asparagus beans directly after burning it over, leaving the stems of suitable size for the vines to run on. In the more open spaces Juan, of his own notion, made any number of *calabaza* hills, and the vines of this superior tropical pumpkin had completely overrun the slope, by the time I was ready to lay off the Mango Avenue.

I headed off and turned aside all that could be saved of the blossoming calabazas, but those exactly in the line of the tree planting had to be sacrificed. On examining the planting more critically, I came to my asparagus beans, and was astonished to find them loaded with green clusters, nearly ready for the table. Before this, I had wondered what could be done with the superabundance of ocra, tomato, egg-plant, sweet pepper, and a host of minor relishes, crowding and overflowing every foot of space around my tent. The coming crop of beans, green corn, cabbages, and sweet potatoes, would be a little fortune to a New York gardener, but here it seemed a question whether I should give them to my neighbors or feed them to Burro, the donkey.

This puzzle received a sudden and satisfactory solution, and that, too, in a way which also settled in my favor the really anxious doubt whether I should be able to clear and fence my twenty acre field in time to realize a crop in December.

Two of my neighbors had promised to assist me in setting up the gate I had constructed to open upon the "New Road" from my enlarged Home Field. But on the morning appointed neither of them came, and Juan failed me also until late in the forenoon. It was hard work for us two, and the harder as we were both unpractised hands, but somehow we had got the posts in, and were tugging at the gate when a young man in sailor garb sauntered up the road with a basket on his arm.

He made a stand at the gateway, whistling a

polka, for a minute or two, with a tantalizing air, and was about turning away when I asked him, in Spanish, to help us adjust the gate on its hinges.

"Don't understand that lingo," he retorted in English, "but I suppose you want me to bear a hand."

Throwing down his basket with the word, he put his shoulder to the gate and soon it swung freely in its place.

The stranger turned out to be a British sailor lately wrecked on this coast, but with the ready adaptability of a thorough tar he had sought and found employment on board the coasting sloop Alice. He was delighted to find a vent for his English tongue and heart, but no more than I was to listen to the outpouring of the flood. He volunteered the information that he was on an independent cruise in search of eggs, plantains, fruits, any thing eatable, in short, for the sloop's crew in part, but mostly, he said, on his own account. The captain had told him that neither fruits nor vegetables were to be bought about Palenque, but he chose to make the attempt, and he added that "having struck a straight road and brought up against a sound bit of English, he had faith in finding a blessed lot of parsnips and potatoes somewhere about."

I could not answer for the parsnips and potatoes under six weeks, but engaged to fill his basket with sundry other vegetables as soon as we had arranged the fastenings for the gate, which by the way, were in hand while this chat was going on.

That done, he went home with me, where the basket was filled and a water-melon for his captain added to the load, after he had tried one on his own account, with an invitation to call for more as often as the Alice came into Palenque. In return, Brent—that is the name he gave himself—promised to bring back on the next trip some trifles I required from Santo Domingo City, and on this we parted, mutually pleased with the encounter.

How Brent reported the affair to Captain Ramirez of the Alice, I am unable to say, but the result was a visit from him to my place in the evening, and a proposal to buy at a fair price all the fruits and vegetables of good class I had to spare for the city market of Santo Domingo.

The winter season had been more than usually dry, and every thing of the kind was in demand. The Alice is making about two trips a week to Santo Domingo and back, coming mainly for satin wood and mahogany, which Don Julio and some of his wealthy friends are shipping to Europe in large quantities. While the Alice is loading, Ramirez collects his little venture of country commodities to sell in the city for his private profit. Hence his proposal to buy my surplus garden-stuff, which came so opportunely to my relief.

The sale of this surplus seems a very trifling matter, but I am not rich enough to despise small things, so I gladly accepted the experiment. Captain Ramirez on his part, sent up a pair of old china crates, and in them, in cool beds of fresh leaves, Juan, Anita, the children, all hands of us, bestirred ourselves to pack the choicest fruits of the garden. Burro made an odd figure with his tall load, travelling down our straight lane to the landing.

Just then my wealthy friend, Don Julio, rode by, and reined up his fine horse, to compliment me on my new gate. He asked with his eyes the destination of this unusual set-out—he is by far too courteous to put the question in words.

I had for a moment the unmanly cowardice to be ashamed of the pettiness of the speculation. A second's thought restored my faltering manhood, and I briefly explained the matter to Don Julio.

"On my word of honor, we of the plains should raise a statue to you, my friend," exclaimed Don Julio, as he reined his horse out of the way of Burro and his load. "This fertile district ought to feed the city of Santo Domingo, as well as half the sugar plantations depending on it, and the striking success of the superior care which you bestow on whatever you cultivate, may teach our people in the rich vales of Palenque how to supply the city market and live in comfort on the profits."

"You are the most encouraging of friends, Don Julio," I answered, opening the gate for him to pass; "but I doubt much whether it will be very profitable to raise vegetables in Palenque, for consumption thirty miles distant at Santo Domingo."

"I assure you that I have no doubt about it—not the shadow of a doubt," replied Don Julio, throwing himself from his horse and leaving his servant in charge of it outside, while he entered the gate with me for a walk through the clearing. He was astonished at the changed appearance of the place, and insisted on hearing in detail every item of my plans.

I led him directly up the broad line, marked off for the Mango Avenue, to the house-site, explaining as we went why, and where, and how, I proposed to carry on my improvements. The questions and remarks of Don Julio were, and ever are, so full of intelligent appreciation and instructive comment, that I always feel clearer and stronger in my course of labors after one of his visits, short as they generally are.

But on that day he was disposed to stay out, and see out, the whole measure of my ambitious projects.

The house-site is covered for the present by a thick carpet of calabaza vines, already gay with great yellow blossoms; but the front is marked out by a range of millet running off on each side of the open space left bare for the Mango Avenue.

On the right, a four-fold row of stakes indicated the pathway to the spring and the places soon to be occupied by my grafted oranges, which, however, I did not intend to move before the end of the month. The projected Orange Walk skirts the beautiful group of fruit-trees, giants of their kind, that have attracted my loving care from the first.

On the left slope, but more to the front, and throwing their broad masses of shade over the house-site, is another magnificent grove of fruit-trees. These were buried in the forest that had grown up around them since the halls of Buena Vista were given to the flames in the negro insurrection, when the estate was abandoned by its masters.

One hesitates to describe the grandeur of these superb trees to persons unacquainted with the majesty of tropical vegetation. When we cleared the wilderness from around them, they towered so far above every thing I had ever seen in an orchard, that they seemed more like the loftiest lords of the forest than the lowlier fruit-bearing servants of civilization. Don Julio smiles at my excessive pride in these trees, but admits that their fruit is agreeable and that they beautify the scene.

Still more to the left, and straggling down to the road, in a picturesque cluster, is, first, an immense tamarind, then two larger but ragged custard apples—which, however, the pruning-knife and saw are gradually reducing to fair proportions—and close upon them, is a group of wild plums, in a line with the fence, and flanking the three almonds newly planted on that side of the gate.

Back of this belt of high, out-spreading trees, is a longer but lower belt of limes, pomegranates, guava and coffee trees. These were only rescued from the encroaching chapparal in February, and yet they are already rich in blossoms and ripening fruit. The guavas have been bearing all the while, though in small quantities, and the plums, also, yielded me more than I and Juan's children could possibly use during March, but their improvement since pruning is marvellous. The limes supply my refreshing noonday beverage, and bid fair, like the guavas and pomegranates, to give plenty of fruit the whole year round.

The guava and pomegranate are, both of them, as healthful as they are palatable, and it is a most agreeable addition to my coarse fare to have these refreshing fruits and my cool lemonade always at command at the mid-day hours of indoor rest.

This fringe of smaller trees and shrubbery is intermingled with some very aged coffee-trees, and the whole is evidently the offspring of the original embellishments of Buena Vista. I am continuing this verdant border in a broad hedge-like sweep around the brow of the eminence and down the slope, until it merges in the "Fruit Grove" on the margin of the spring. There it will join the Orange Walk, that is to be, and complete a circle of ever-blossoming ever-bearing, fruit-trees, not less than four hundred yards in circuit.

Even now the only considerable break in the line of shade is on the slope between what I have named the Spring Grove and the beginning of the Guava Thicket, and even that fragment of open space is partially filled by two trees standing side by side, apart from the rest, and in superb contrast with each other. One is an old bread-fruit tree, somewhat tattered when I first saw it, but now tossing abroad its great bright green leaves like banners of pride, amid the deep glossy foliage of the tall *guanabana* at its side. The guanabana lavished its refreshing fruit of "consolidated lemonade" all through February and March, but it ceased bearing in April, and went into an extravagant profusion of queer little buds which, by courtesy have to be accepted as blossoms, and which will not ripen into fruit before mid summer.

The custard-apple and guanabana fill the space between the *caimete*—which abounds in February and March—and the mango, which is the rich and generous gift of June and July. The orange runs from September to May, but it is not plentiful in the first and last months of its regular season. There are oranges of some kinds all the year, but the Dominican season for the large, unequalled "sweet orange" is mainly included in the seven months between September and May. All the other months have their own rich and varied fruits, and my trees in April and May have been peculiarly bounteous in custard-apples and guanabanas, in addition to several other fruits which are continuing on from January, February, and March, to the present moment.

If I dwell too much on the charms of my tropical fruit groves, and on the labors of love I devote to them, Don Julio Perez should bear half the censure. Whenever he breaks into Buena Vista he forces me away from every thing else to look at and talk about them. Two or three times a week he rides over or sends a servant with something new to plant, which perhaps he has obtained miles away.

I had noted in my diary twenty kinds of fruit-bearing trees and shrubs, already here in maturity or lately transplanted, when on this, the very last working day of the month, he rushed upon me in the midst of a rainy afternoon with a donkey load of plantain and banana roots. Juan received them in dismay, for he had just finished setting out a row of pine-apples which he had found running wild in an abandoned cane-field, and wanted to go home. Don Julio would not hear of it, until the plantains were all in the ground. His own servant was directed to take a hoe, and every man of us had to bend to the work while the light lasted. I fancy Don Julio never before did so much manual labor in one day since he was born, but he held to it bravely till the last banana was fairly settled in the bosom of mother earth, by the fading twilight. Then he began to rally me on "wasting so much time and trouble in getting so much more than enough of what nature alone would supply in sufficiency, without vexing the earth with extra cares."

Yet these "extra cares" have certainly more than doubled the fruit yield of Buena Vista, and on every arrival of the Alice from Santo Domingo, Captain Ramirez calls for more than I can supply, both of fruit and vegetables.

With a thankful heart I note, that even the little I have done, and am doing, in these small matters, has relieved my mind of a most anxious doubt as to the feasibility of clearing and fencing the twenty acre lot, in season to plant a crop for December.

These little labors are paying for my large clearing. The garden returns are not magnificent. A Russian Prince or still less, an army contractor might not regard it as an important additiou to his revenues, but to me it was a precious step towards an early, though humble independence.

It enabled me to hire two experienced native woodmen to cut down the timber, and make ready the fencing for my new field, while I went on with the lighter labors of my fruit and garden work: and in that too, it gave me the means to pay a stout, serviceable man to assist during the latter part of the month in completing the planting and other improvements in my "Home Lot," including the garden.

Thus I have had three laborers for two-thirds of the busy month of May, in return for my own industry and "extra efforts."

The "New Field" is rough and bristling with the stumps of the felled woodlands, but my Home Lot is one wide, waving landscape of rich-toned verdure; and again at the close of this month, I add the last page to my notes for May, with devout thanks to the All-Giver for his manifold bounties.

CHAPTER VII.

JUNE.

Rapid growth of vegetation.—No labor equal to white labor.—What machinery will do in the tropics.—National bread of the Island.—Description of the *cassava* and the *arapa.*—Indian fashion of baking.—Yuca and yams.—Delightful visit from Delfino.—He discovers a new treasure.—A spirited discussion.—Resolve to maintain my "humble independence."—Delfino proposes an October banquet.—Where to come off.—Am greatly surprised.—Visit to the wood-cutters.—Delfino's anger.—An unhappy discovery.—How the difficulty is arranged.—Mahogany.—Satin-wood.—A new cottage resolved on.—How it was planned.

THE rapid growth of vegetation almost exceeds belief. Twice in May, and again in June, I had to run the donkey "weeder" through and through every corn row. Ten or twelve days were sufficient to cover the ground again with a green carpet of weeds and springing grass. My neighbors assured me that one such thorough weeding was enough, but I was not of their opinion; I wanted the whole strength of the sun and soil for the full development of the children of my care, and they have repaid me generously.

Those who say the treasures of the tropics are to be best won by the brute force of ignorant labor, cannot have studied with sufficient patience the march of invention.

Intelligent laborers; men who know how to make wood and iron perform the severest part, to the sparing of human sinews; men who can work steam in harness, these are what is wanted here.

Those, too, are mistaken who fancy that no skin but a black one can cover the firm muscle and vigorous endurance of a perfect and hardy manhood. *The most manly workers I have seen in this country are white men.* I will not cite my well-born and wealthy friend, Delfino, because he is not habitually a working man, but apart from him the few who have good farms of their own tilling are mostly white men. They and they only know how to obtain and *use* the best class of labor-saving machines, and they are too prudent to trust any one but themselves to manage them, for they know that superior implements, and the recklessness of brute force don't work well together. Under the warm sun of the tropics, *intelligent working men and machinery will yet open the grandest field of civilization* ever realized.

Even in such a small matter as hoeing a corn-field, this is illustrated. Without violent labor I do as much clearing in a short forenoon with my little donkey cultivator as three good field-hands will accomplish in the whole day, and do the work much more effectually. Rating Burro and myself as equal to a pair of Dominicans, the cultivator, which neither eats, sulks, nor runs away (to which as a class *they* are subject), counts for four common hands, which are subject to all those defects—the cultivator, I repeat, fairly counts for four laborers and asks no wages. It must also be remembered that, over and above the gain in time, the crops are better in quality, and far more secure from extremes of rain and drought, for the well and deeply stirred soil affords the roots ease and space to bury themselves out of reach of danger.

Captain Ramirez gives the best price for my fruits, as well as for my melons, corn, beans, ocra, tomatoes, and vegetables generally, not only because, to use his own words, "there is enough of them to be worth coming for, but on account of their fine size and condition, which excels any thing to be seen from other fields, not even excepting those of the fertile plains of Palenque."

The corn ears are now so full and forward that I am cutting them—and at so near the close of the month I may say I *have* cut them, as fast as the kernels were well glazed. The housewives of Santo Domingo prefer it at this stage of ripeness, for making that most delicate of hoe-cakes, *arapa*. Thus my five acres of corn have netted me, outside of my own labor, but including the price of Burro—I paid for him just sixteen dollars—a clear two hundred dollars. This two hundred dollars, minus the sixteen, leaves me sufficient to pay for a milch cow and a strong working mule, and I have yet a surplus to cover the thatching of my new work-room. But as that is not yet half built, we will leave it to its own proper season, and turn back to the national *breads* of this island.

The Spanish conquerors found two excellent varieties of bread in great plenty among the natives of Hayti, and the Indian names, as well as the articles, continue in popular use to this day. One kind is the *cassava*, which is made of the bulbous root of the yuca, ground and baked in large thin cakes; the other is the *arapa*, which is composed of young corn mixed with an equal quantity of cocoa-nut grated fresh. The whole is moistened to a proper consistency by the milk of the cocoa-nut, and then folded in banana leaves and baked before the fire, which is the Indian fashion of bread-baking, from snowy Maine to burning Yucatan, before and since the advent of the white race.

It is not difficult for a farmer here to keep up a succession of corn and yuca crops during the entire year, and one man's labor might easily feed a hundred persons, not merely with *cassava* and *arapa*, but with as large and as palatable a variety of fruits, grains, and vegetables as can be found, whether native or naturalized, in any one section of the habitable globe.

Yuca and yams are the equivalents of the Northern potatoes for table use, and, under a system of thorough ploughing, are still more profitable crops than corn, but they require a much longer time for ripening. My corn was in market in three months from the planting, but the yuca will require from six to eight months, and the yams will not be ripe under nine or ten months.

Next to cotton, and better than sugar, taking one year with another, is a good yam crop, but its enormous roots require deep ploughing, such as Americans provide for their potatoes to expand in. But that is what no one in this country thinks of, and, consequently, there is no such thing here as a respectable yam field.

I planted about sixty hills for my own supply, and Juan says I will have to take them out with a "stump puller," they will run so deep in the soft ground broken up by the ox plough.

Juan has made a friendly acquaintance with the

plough and cultivator, but the "*Stump Extractor*" he cannot get within the grasp of his comprehension, although in answer to his anxious inquiries I have labored diligently to explain how it manages to persuade the stumps out of the embraces of Mother Earth.

This month has been brightened by a visit from Delfino. He came down to Palenque to receive a sugar mill and other machinery which he had ordered from the United States. Besides his own ever-welcome self, he brought back my heavy plough in time for me to plant yuca in the ground from which I am cutting off the earliest corn. His cheering helpfulness and his judicious, intelligent experience are to my soul what these June showers and sunshine are to my labors—life and youth.

I could offer him a slightly improved table, for I have now chickens, eggs, and a milch goat to help out our fare, but he would not stop in-doors long enough to take more than a slice of water-melon, he was in such a hurry to see what I had accomplished in his absence.

We went first to the house-site, by the new Orange Walk, then on to the gate by the Mango Avenue, and back through the circular border of mingled fruits to the spring grove by the tent. The frequent afternoon rains—it seldom rains in the forenoon at any season of the year in this part of Santo Domingo—but the abundant evening showers had brought out every thing beautifully, and all the place wore its brightest and freshest looks.

The green corn stalks yet waved their long leaves in their places, for Captain Ramirez had bargained for them with a stable keeper in Santo Domingo, and the time of delivery was yet ten days ahead. The walks were green with close cut grass, the little travel they had, barely marking a path in the centre.

"What an immensity of work has been done here," said Delfino gazing up and down the clearing. "You have several hands now, Julio tells me."

"Only two, and they are in the woodland clearing my new field," I answered. "My garden and cornfield have turned out so well, that I can employ two men steadily with the proceeds, but I keep them at cutting timber and making fence. I have had a third man part of the time in this home lot, but mainly to assist in laying out the ground and planting the trees."

"I should think it fair work for one man to keep the weeds and grass cut down so close and even in these broad walks. They take up considerable room," said Delfino, as he turned back towards the hut.

"Burro does not find the walks too extensive," I answered, smiling at Delfino's Dominican ideas of wasting land.

"Why surely you do not allow the donkey to run in them among your tender trees?" he asked in surprise.

"Certainly not. I know very well that Burro would browse off my young trees in a day. There he is, you see, picketed under those large fruit-trees by the spring, and I will show you how he is interested in the breadth of the walks."

Taking down the strong bladed "weed scythe"

which I had brought with me, I mowed the grass off a few yards of the walk, and this, with half a dozen blades of corn, made Burro's meal.

Delfino seized the scythe before I could hang it in its place, poised and swayed it in the idle air for a moment, and then made at the grassy walk with such a vigorous demonstration that I was soon obliged to interfere.

"There, that will do, Delfino," I said, laying strong hands on the scythe, "you have cut enough for Burro's breakfast and dinner to-morrow, and he likes his herb supper perfectly fresh. Even a donkey prefers fresh food to stale."

"Very well, I give it up now, but I claim the right, as your pupil, you know, to cut all the grass Burro eats while I am here. I must learn how to use this admirable novelty."

How strange to me this term "novelty," for a common scythe. Yet in this country it is, in very truth, something entirely new.

"In learning to use it, my dear Delfino, you must also learn how to take care of it, and keep it in order, or it will soon be good for nothing. Delfino assented, and we went through the whole process of grinding and whetting it before he would sit down to supper.

In the morning I gave him a practical lesson with the scythe, by allowing him to mow the fringe of grass and weeds along the fence. The grass in all the walks is specially reserved for Burro, and is freshly cut bit by bit, for him when he is kept up for work. By the time I have gone over them all, from end to end, in this piecemeal way, the grass has started up so well at the place of beginning, that I can begin over again to repeat the cutting.

Delfino came to breakfast much exhilarated with his success in handling the scythe. He wonders much, and so do I, that this simple yet efficient implement has never been introduced in Santo Domingo.

"You Americans know how to make wood and steel do three-quarters of your work in every thing, and that is the reason why you are not afraid to undertake so much of it," said Delfino. "Your improvements here are, in truth, miraculous."

"I assure you, Delfino, that any American farmer

would think very lightly of this small pattern of a place, and none, but a very poor one, like myself, would be contented with such a limited showing for a crop. I, however, am satisfied and grateful, for, with nothing but my own hands and this moderate outfit of farming implements, I believe myself in a fair way to achieve a real though humble independence—thanks to you, my friend, and to Don Julio."

"Thanks to nobody!" exclaimed Delfino quickly. "You have your homestead secured, and enough even now coming out of the ground to support you. But let me tell you, *amigo mio*, that first of all things, you must build a house. Your tent will not hold out this rainy season."

"It *must* do, Delfino, this year, at least. It ought to be good enough for me, when no better tents are the only shelter of thousands of gallant men who perhaps are less inured to hardship than I am."

"That is no reason why you—and they, too, for that matter— should not have houses when they can be had," replied Delfino.

"In my case, a house *cannot* be had," I answered,

decidedly. "My first care is to improve my fields and create the means for a sure and steady support. Meanwhile this shelter will serve my purpose."

"I see you have gained another step towards independence. You are raising your own breadstuffs," said Delfino, abruptly turning the conversation, and pouncing upon the hot *arapa* which Anita brought in with the omelet and coffee.

While we were at breakfast, Anita, my infallible reliance on company occasions, was on duty, and her fresh corn cakes justified the pleasant pride she manifested in them.

"Yes, I now raise my own bread and corn," I replied, "and in due time I hope to have a regular abundance of cassava."

"I glanced at your yuca while I was mowing, and it seems uncommonly forward," said Delfino. "Prince Plough and General Weeder have fairly buried Miss Yuca under their magnificent bounties. She is now rich, and invites me to a banquet of fresh cassava, in—let us reflect—yes, we may say, in October, is it not so, *mi amigo?*"

"Certainly," I answered, laughing. "The first cassava cake from my own fields, the first pair of chickens and the first fatling kid of my own raising, shall be kept to grace your welcome."

"Thank you, and please add to them the first arrow-root custard, and the first glass of ginger-wine made from your own garden? I stipulate for these also," persisted Delfino, with a comically serious air.

"Good! The arrow-root custard shall not be wanting; neither shall the ginger-wine, though I confess I have not the faintest idea in what way I shall manufacture it."

"Oh, if the wit to make it don't come to you by nature—and it seems to me the art to do every thing they choose to do is born with the Yankees," laughed Delfino, "our Julio's mayoral will teach you how to make it. He has an extraordinary capacity for producing our country wines—and a greater one for drinking them—but you need not be too exacting with him about that part of it," he added, rising from the table.

"Oh, you may count on the wine also, Delfino; I

will accomplish it," I said, as I followed him to the outside of the tent.

"But neither the cassava, nor the custard, nor the wine is to be thought of in any other place than your new house. Understand that perfectly, *amigo mio*, I must find you in the new house, and nowhere else, on my next visit, or we shall have words about it."

"My new house, Delfino! You must be dreaming. A new house in October is, for me, simply an impossibility, unless, indeed, you have brought Aladdin's lamp in your pocket."

Delfino lit his cigar and deigned no further reply. Presently he came up whistling to assist me in getting Burro in gear for his and my morning trip to the woodlands, and when all was ready we started off merrily together for a forenoon of earnest work.

Most of my June afternoons were demanded at the home lot, but three or four hours of the morning had to be regularly devoted to the wood-cutters.

Sometimes a fine tree for house timber had to be spared for future use; sometimes I had to handle my heavy American axe to cut a tree close to the ground, and then measure off the timber, to suit my particular purpose.

It was always necessary to watch over these men, if I wished to keep the fence line clear, and have the materials piled in fit and accessible order. I have no taste for doing the same thing twice over, but both of my men seemed to have a genius for leaving every cutting in the way of the next day's work, so that without constant superintendence one-half of their time would be lost in lifting and removing obstacles created by their own careless management.

On that morning we were hardly inside the clearing when I saw an uneasy, displeased look cross the usually open and sunny brow of my friend Delfino.

With a frown, he walked over and around the heaps of wood, scanning the timber and questioning the men with a closeness that surprised me. I was hauling, that is, I was loading and driving, and patient Burro was hauling away, some fence-posts of more than needful length and solidity, when Delfino (whom I had left talking to the wood-cutters) suddenly put his hand on my shoulder and said, mockingly:

"You are a helpless innocent, and I must take you in charge."

"I appreciate your kindness, but how long is it since it has pleased you to exchange the character of pupil for that of guardian?" I asked with some surprise.

"Only now, and only in part," he answered with a smile. "You shall still be my master in the realms of cultivation, but I must be yours in the forest, where timber is the only harvest."

"So be it; but tell me why you are so warm about it. There is, of course, a reason for this decided resolution."

"I want to make a contract for building you a snug little country cottage," said Delfino, dashing off at his own good pleasure from the subject before us. "I want to build for you, not a palace, but a plain, comfortable shelter at a fair price, and I will take my pay in satin-wood."

"Build cottage or palace as you please, Delfino.

It is all one to me this year. Consult your own taste as to the extent of the edifice and its style of architecture. I should be sorry to cripple your genius with base conditions. I will allow you the same unlimited charter to pay yourself, if you can discover the means, for I give you notice that I shall never again attempt to oppose any proposition of yours, however ridiculous or impracticable."

"Let Burro alone for three minutes, and answer me seriously one question," said Delfino, planting himself before the donkey so that I could not turn him.

I regarded him with increased surprise as he went on:

"Will you give up to me your miserable tent and all the satin-wood in this clearing, if I will have a cottage built for you equal to that of Manuel the carpenter, on the Savanna? Yes or no?"

"Yes, with all my heart, as to the satin-wood. But for the miserable tent—no, I cannot spare that for the present, my friend."

"Enough. I accept the satin-wood, and offer my

humble apology to the tent. I did not apply the epithet 'miserable' to that most respectable institution; on the contrary, I esteem it excessively. I may say I adore it—in dry weather; I intended merely to signify that your whim to live in it through the rainy season, is miserable enough. I hope that is satisfactory."

"Perfectly, my dear Delfino, except that I don't in the least understand your meaning in all this outbreak about satin-wood and a cottage."

"The meaning of it all is, that these fellows have taken advantage of your inexperience in precious woods, to steal a fine lot for themselves. Here, for example, is a stump of satin-wood," putting his foot on it as he spoke. "There are two more, partly hidden by the brush thrown over them, and I am confident that we shall find a dozen more under those piles of trash."

"But where can the wood be?" I asked, in bewilderment. "I am here almost every day, and do the most part of the piling and hauling myself, and I cannot imagine how these men found an opportunity to cut and carry away any amount of wood worth mentioning."

"They found time in the afternoons. They noticed that you seldom came here except in the mornings, and they cut and carried off, far enough to hide in the after-part of the day, every valuable piece they had previously spied out."

"But what can I do about it? How can I recover it? I cannot begin my career in this country by criminal prosecutions. You surely would not advise me, a stranger, to adopt sudden and harsh measures with these poor men, who, with their families, are, after all, my neighbors?"

"Perhaps not," said Delfino. "Leave Julio and I to manage the affair. We are both forest owners, and have a strong interest in the suppression of wood thieves. We understand the class, and shall know how to bring these rascals to confession without soiling our hands with those expensive nuisances—courts and prisons."

"But, Delfino, I really cannot consent to your taking so much trouble on my account! I had rather let the affair pass in silence, and get other wood-choppers to finish my work, than have a stir about it."

"There, stop talking, my dear innocent, while I set you right," put in Delfino in his abrupt, positive way. "In the first place, it is not *your* business but *mine.* You have sold me the wood for a new cottage. In the second, you cannot get other woodcutters as easily as you fancy; and thirdly, there will be no stir; for we, that is, Julio and I, will make the rogues disgorge under promise of pardon and secrecy. Nothing will be exacted of them for this offence, if they go on well with their chopping and sin no more."

I thanked Delfino heartily for his kind and judicious intervention, and promised to leave every thing in his hands.

"Even the new cottage?" he said, archly.

"Have I not promised *never* again to resist you?"

"That is most wisely resolved, *amigo miò,*" cried out Delfino, in great glee; "for in that, more than any thing else, I had firmly determined to have my own way. But now that you are in such a promising frame of mind, we will go home to dinner."

During our noon-tide rest we talked over the cottage plan, and shaped out the course of work until we were of nearly one mind at all points.

In this unexpected manner was I decided to begin building, months in advance of my most sanguine hopes. But I have not adopted Delfino's plan of a cottage, like that of the rich carpenter on the prairie. His house is not precisely what would suit me to see on the site of Buena Vista, and yet it is much too expensive for me to venture upon while my homestead is not wholly paid for, and while I am yet so deficient in dairy and working stock for my farm. All this I had to argue with Delfino, point by point, until we gradually came to agree.

I conceded that it was best to build something in the way of shelter at once, and Delfino admitted that with my "monomania," as he styled my intense dread of going beyond my means, it was well enough not to attempt any thing expensive. I consented to devote all the satin-wood of the clearing to the new cottage, but only after the balance due Don Julio on the homestead should be paid. I had previously reserved three fine mahogany trees, growing near the line of the fence, for this purpose, and these, with whatever other cabinet woods we might meet in levelling the forest, would, I had promised myself, be more than sufficient to wipe out the debt. Delfino's discovery of the satin-wood had presented speedier and more abundant means than I had ventured to expect, but still I would not encroach upon them until an unencumbered homestead was secure.

This has been my thought by day and my dream by night, during years of struggle in that busy, dusty, far-off city of my loathing. The dwelling would soon come of itself, I felt sure, whenever I had so far advanced that a fair space for free and willing labor should be fully, firmly, unquestionably *my own.*

Before Delfino returned home, the cottage was finely under way. He had made our dishonest woodcutters give up more than three thousand feet of superior satin-wood worth on the spot fifty dollars the thousand, which they had managed to convey to the vicinity of the weighing wharf at Palenque Bay, and hid under the brush and sand. More than three thousand feet of a somewhat inferior character was thrown by in the heaps of fencing stuff, in the hope, probably, that I would overlook it in my ignorance of the appearance and value of the precious woods.

Don Julio bought it all, and would gladly have bought ten times as much for freight to Europe. After deducting the balance due him, he sent me a note stating that he held one hundred and eighty dollars at my order. One hundred and eighty dollars is a slight thing to him, a trifle to be noted in his business books and forgotten in the next hour, but small as it is, it will build me a snug cottage.

Insignificant as it may be, I enter into it with a feeling that within its shelter I am its master and my own—a sentiment of joy and independence not to be exchanged for life in a palace, if that life and that palace are ruled at the will of another.

CHAPTER VIII.

JULY.

My palenca.—Active preparations.—Kindness of Delfino and Don Julio.—Manuel, the carpenter.—Description of my new cottage.—A sudden apparition.—Tio Juanico.—Sanchez, the limeburner.—Juanico's history.—Engage him to work for me. —His mysterious disappearance.—Is he faithless?—Abrupt return.—Juanico wounded.—His distress.—What I do for him.—Cost of building.—The sea-breeze.—Fourth of July, how we celebrate it.—The grand feast.—Yuca and yautilia.—My corn crop.—Abounding wealth of vegetables.

ON first entering upon my wild homestead, I had not dreamed of attempting to build any thing in the shape of a better dwelling than the old cabin, under eight or ten months at least. I did not dare hope that my best exertions could produce from this bit of wilderness the means, even then, for erecting more than a rude and temporary shelter. But the wholesome, faith-inspiring visit of Delfino opened a brighter prospect.

On calculating cost, and weighing carefully the means, my own labor included, I became of Delfino's opinion, about the middle of June—as I noted in my record of the month—that I could afford to build a snug, cleanly, and durable "*palenca*," cottage, which would answer the immediate purpose of a dwelling. In the event of being able to build a more commodious house on the chosen site of Buena Vista, this cottage would finally serve for the very necessary farm appendage of tool-house, and workshop.

The evening after Delfino came to his conclusion about the value of the satin-wood taken from the new clearing, we called on Don Julio and all three of us went seriously and solemnly into the discussion of the size, and the corresponding estimates, for the new cottage. Before we slept it was agreed that it could be built for one hundred dollars, except the floors and carpenter work.

The next morning we selected and measured off the building place on the slope, shaded by my favorite Fruit Grove; the front looking up the Orange

Walk to the crest of Buena Vista, and the rear opening in the direction of the spring.

While I went to the "clearing" to look after my more than suspected wood-choppers, Delfino made another visit to Don Julio, and, as I learned afterwards by his success, asked and induced that kind friend to send over three of his best hands, to assist us in "house raising."

The space marked out was only fourteen by twenty-four feet—people don't expect to build immensely on a capital of one hundred dollars—but that allows me two modest little rooms. We measured the spaces, and with Juan's help dug the holes and set the upright posts; allowing duly for doorways front and rear, and a window at each end. The doors and windows to fill these places were to be the subject of consideration at a future day. Sufficient for the present, and our allotted one hundred dollars, were the roof and walls of our much-discussed, and to me deeply interesting cottage.

The carpenter from Savana Grande was brought over to assist in hewing and fitting the "plat" timbers which surmount the uprights and support the rafters. Manuel, the carpenter, is a man of substance, and holds himself of no mean importance in the little prairie village of Savana Grande, but Delfino hurried him about with as much impetuosity as if we were all engaged in erecting a royal pavillion, which must, let who may suffer, be ready for kingly occupation at a given moment.

Manuel yielded to the delusion of a life and death urgency, when he saw gentlemen like Don Julio and Don Delfino working with me side by side, handling tools, moving timber, and making themselves useful generally, in the midst of their own servants. Such distinguished countenance, covered me and my "*palenca*" with dignity, and the honest carpenter allowed himself to be driven about as he had never submitted to be driven before. But then, my friends were men of distinction, while his ordinary employers were common people, who only paid by the day.

Palenca is the old Indian name for a peculiar kind of house, made of rough lathing, split from small branches, and closely woven between posts set in the ground. The woven walls are plastered over, inside and out, with mud or mortar, and are as neat as they are cheap. These "palencas" are covered with a tall pyramid roof of palm thatching, or sometimes with the same woven and plastered sheeting that composes the side-walls, and when the whole is whitewashed in its own peculiar style, it has a very quaint, picturesque effect.

My new cottage was to be a thatched palenca, and as soon as the posts were set and the rafters on, Juan went into the village on the prairie, to engage all the thatchers and lathmen he could collect, in order to follow up the work with the better speed. Thatch and thatchers we soon had, and the roof was up and finished ten days after the raising; but the lathsplitters kept disappointing me, and the sides of the palenca were filled up with tedious slowness.

It is the busy time for planting and hoeing, and the men would not leave their own home work for mine in the woods at the ordinary wages. They are the less willing to do so, as in this season the laborer is likely to be caught out in the sudden and violent showers now common in the afternoons. The mornings, however, are almost invariably fine, as I have had occasion to state in the preceding months, and counting on this agreeable peculiarity of the climate, I followed up my woodland work very closely in the forenoons, and snatched the clear afternoon intervals, when they offered, for my garden.

The day that Delfino was busy with me and my two woodmen in selecting the uprights for the cottage, a man of singular appearance silently dropped in on us from some by-path. No one seemed to know or notice him, until Delfino looked up and held out his hand with a warm smile of welcome.

"Ah, my good Tio Juanico, is that you? I rejoice to see you here," said Delfino, in his sunny, cordial way. "I hope you are as healthy and as happy as ever."

"I am always well, and at your service, *mi señor*," the man answered with manifest pleasure. "I heard you were on a visit at Don Julio's, and I went there to salute you. Don Julio's people told me you were with Señor Vecino, and I went to the tent, but found no one at home. Then I went to Juan's, and he directed me here."

"You have had a long walk, Tio Juanico," said Delfino, kindly. "Where do you live now?"

"I work for Sanchez, the lime-burner, on the Nizao river; but his last kiln for the season is made, and I have no wages now."

"Then you have come in good time, Juanico; the Señor is looking for lathmen to get out the stuff and help build his palenca. Can you begin work to-day?" asked Delfino.

"Si Señor. This moment, if you please."

"That is talking like a man, my good Tio," returned Delfino. Take your knife and pull the bark from these house-posts. When they are done, you may do the same for the rafters, but that will be for to-morrow."

At the word, Tio Juanico drew the long knife which the country people always carry at their belts, and applied himself to work with an air of steady and composed satisfaction, while I paused for a moment to study this new addition to my force.

His dark Indian face, with its gentle mouth and sadly earnest eyes, was not uncomely, and his shapely head, with its mass of jetty hair, was really noticeable in its fine proportions, but both his back and breast had a peculiar and ungainly prominence, amounting to deformity. Aside from this, he was a muscular, well-limbed man, in the strength of his age, and, as I soon saw, as ready as he was capable for hard work. His voice was strikingly clear and musical, but it had the same expression of patient sadness which looked out of his eyes.

In the hurry of the hour I thought no more about him, but when noon came, and I was starting home with a load of posts with Burro, I called Tio Juanico to come with us and get some dinner. At night, Delfino suggested that our new man should sleep near him in the old cabin. There was nothing there in the shape of bed or bedding, for Delfino occupied the hammock, but he cut for himself a few branches, and with an armful of corn-leaves arranged a couch to his entire content. The poor fellow had given away his blanket to a sick man at the lime-kiln—so Juan told us—and literally had little more than he stood in, on the face of the earth. He had formerly been in Delfino's employ, but his fellow-servants had treated him so unkindly that he could not endure to stay. When pressed by Delfino to name his persecutors, he declined doing so, choosing rather to leave his place than cause the dismissal of his inconsiderate tormentors.

So Juanico drifted down to the Nizao, and thence to me at the moment when Delfino, having forced me to build, was on the look-out for help to forward the work. Delfino's sketch of his character, and Juan's account of his kindness to his sick friend, prepossessed me in Juanico's favor, and I was right glad to have him with me while Delfino prolonged his visit.

All the next day and the next one after, Juanico worked quietly and faithfully in preparing the house timber. The third was the "raising day," and he did not spare himself from daylight to dark, but at night he suddenly disappeared. He had asked me at noon, if I should require him after the frame was up, and I answered by engaging him for another week for the lath splitting and weaving. He then entreated the favor of an advance of three days' wages, besides what was already due, and I gave it to him without hesitation, for, even without Delfino's testimony in favor of his strict honesty, I would have trusted his candid face for a much larger sum.

In the evening of the "raising" he was missing. Still we thought little about his absence, but when a whole day passed, and Delfino—whom he knew was to return home at that time—had to start without seeing him, my confidence in Tio Juanico was slightly abated. This was Saturday, and as I sat in the dark of the evening, thinking of the void which the departure of Delfino's sunny spirit leaves in my solitary dwelling-place, gazing into the obscurity at the meteor flittings of the fire-flies—a little lonely, and much fatigued with the incessant labors of the week, Tio Juanico startled me by noiselessly gliding along and standing before me, as mute as a statue, actually unseen until within a distance of six feet.

"I thought you had left altogether, Juanico," I

said, coldly. "Your good friend, Don Delfino, was surprised that you were not here when he went away."

"Oh! Señor excuse me," said Juanico, humbly. "I met with an accident. My hand is lame. I cannot be of any use to you now, but when my hand is better, I will, with your permission, come and work out what I owe you. I will work for you until you are satisfied."

"All the work I wish you to do will probably be finished before your hand is well," I answered, with increased coldness.

"Then I will work for somebody else, Señor, and bring you the money, for I am not lazy, nor dishonest. It makes the heart pain more than the hand, to have Don Delfino and the Señor think badly of me."

He uttered this in a low, imploring tone that went home to my better self.

"What is the matter with your hand, Juanico?" I asked, in a softened tone.

"I went to see a sick friend at Rio Nizao. He

was dying and wanted the priest. I went for him, and, to be quick, I rode a wild young horse. In returning, the horse started and dashed me amongst the trees, and hurt my arm."

He stopped short with a suppressed sigh of pain, that I fancied came indeed more from the heart than the hand.

"Let me look at your hand," I said, turning into the tent to light the lamp. He had it in his bosom, and he held it out to me, supported in the other. I saw the wrist was sprained and badly swollen. I did what I could to relieve it. I bathed and bandaged it, after rubbing the whole arm with olive tar, the liniment of my special faith, and then contrived a sling to protect the injured member and leave the other at liberty.

While I was busy with this I happened to meet his eye, and was struck with its look of subdued anguish. It was not the expression of physical pain, it was the deep grief of the soul, written with a painful distinctness, such as I have rarely seen inscribed on any human countenance.

He dropped his eyes to the ground as he met my earnest, questioning glance.

"Let us hope, Tio Juanico, that your friend is happier where he is than he could be with us."

I uttered this common-place to start the iron pressure upon the heart of the poor mourner, and force him to speak, perhaps to weep, that the pent-up tide might flow out and relieve him, but he only bent his head in silence.

"Was he a near relation, Juanico?"

"My cousin. I never had brother or sister. José was my only friend." He uttered the words sadly and slowly, but almost firmly, and turned to leave the tent.

I allowed him to escape into the friendly obscurity of the evening outside, but there I stopped him with his *adios* on his lips.

"There is a hammock for you, Juanico, which Don Delfino left on your account, in the old cabin, and if you choose to remain with me until your hand is cured we will see about work afterwards."

He stood a moment without speaking, and then

with the one word *gracias*—thanks—he hastily entered the cabin as if to busy himself in the dark. Half an hour later I went there to offer him some supper, but he begged to be excused, and bidding him good-night I left him alone with his grief.

I am habitually an early riser, but Tio Juanico was up before me, and had prepared the coffee and toasted cassava, to hand me as soon as I was ready to take it. I dressed his arm again and found him able to slightly bend his fingers, so that I could assure him that no bone was out of place. From that hour he seemed to have no thought but how best to serve my interests.

How he managed to do so much with one hand I cannot imagine. I left him plying the splint broom about the tent, when I went to the clearing for a load of lathing, and when I returned, somewhat before noon, he was busy in the garden, helping one of Captain Ramirez' men to pack a load of fruit and vegetables for the city. The thatch, the cane, and the vine cords for tying them, had come in while I was in the forest, and Juanico had attended to that also, while directing and assisting the thatchers about the roof arrangements. This work being peculiar to the country, he had managed it much better than I could have done, for the whole business was familiar to him and new to me.

All the week he watched faithfully over the thatchers, and but for him they would not have completed the work in the time agreed upon with Delfino. When not engaged with them, he would take a turn in the field or garden to note the state of the crop, and single out what was fit for market, and have all ready to deliver to Captain Ramirez when the Alice came in for cargo.

Whatever Tio Juanico was clearly and patiently instructed how to do, was thereafter done in exact time and method, whether about the house or grounds. I soon learned that I had unwittingly secured a most faithful help in this time of need. For without omitting a single day my careful attention to the wood-cutting, the cottage went on, and the garden was not neglected, under his unwearied care.

The frame of my *palenca* had occupied me a week, getting it out and setting it up, and the roofing-in consumed another week.

Two men in one day tied on the rafters, and on these rafters the lattice of reeds for the support of the palm-leaf thatching, and the same men put on the thatch in three days more. On Thursday it rained, and they went home in the afternoon, leaving the peak of the roof unfinished.

These men did not come back to finish it until Saturday afternoon, when we closed accounts. They were to do the work and find the tying vines for eight dollars, but, looking to durability, I agreed to add another dollar, and have the thatch put on with extra closeness and care. The palm-leaves, as agreed for by Delfino, came to a trifle less than nine dollars, and the reeds to a trifle more than one dollar—ten dollars for all the material—so the roof cost me just nineteen dollars.

The north end and a portion of the west side were filled in with the woven lathing, without the use of a nail, almost as soon as the roof was done, but there the "siding-up" stopped for some days. I was put off from day to day by the men who had undertaken this part of the palenca, but who would work a part of one day, and then be off for the next two, until my patience was more than exhausted.

Delfino had promised to spend the ever-glorious Fourth of July with me, and I was anxious to receive him in the new cottage. The men who had thatched it were finally induced by Tio Juanico to go into the woods and assist in getting out the lathing, and with great exertions and some additional expense, three sides of the cottage were closed in by the evening of the third of July. The south front was still open, and what to do about it, was the subject of much serious consultation between my old friend Juan, my new man Juanico, and myself.

My accommodating tent settled the whole difficulty at last. I slept in it the night of the third, but I was up with the dawn, and by eight in the morning, we had removed the tent and its belongings to the new cottage. With very little arrangement it made a partition between the rooms, and a convenient front curtain to screen the privacy of my future bed-chamber.

On the Fourth, I was truly and happily in a house of my own, and the sense of space and comfort it offered was a positive luxury, after my months of cramped quarters in my old lodging. Yet, truth to say, I thought very little about these inconveniences while I was absorbed in the greater necessity of getting my ground and crops in safe progress.

The larger portion of my palenca is still open to the south, but that side is delightfully overarched by the thick branches of my fruit-trees. The welcome sea-breeze plays freely through their majestic trunks, but their green, never-fading foliage protects the room from the sun, and even the rain, almost like a roof.

It has the free and open freshness of an arbor, with almost the security of a close and finished room. I am adding a kind of kitchen at the end, which it is intended to veil with a screen of flowering vines. Already I am beginning to find a little time and place for the ornamental.

On the Fourth, Julio and Delfino came together, somewhat later in the day than I had expected, but they were after all in good season and warmly welcomed.

I was proud to receive them in my airy, rustic bower, and not ashamed of the simple dinner Anita set before them. There is always abundance of fine fish in Palenque Bay, and the dish of the occasion was a real American chowder, provided for them according to an old promise, at their own special request. I had hoarded up the last of my Boston crackers and other little matters from home for my first "Independence Day" in this new land of promise, and the feast was all the better relished for being laid out in the cool, delicious shade of my open-fronted but tree-embowered *palenca.*

Other dishes on our genial, gipsy board, were to *me* as acceptable novelties as my friends declared the Yankee chowder to be to *them.* Tio Juanico, whose hand and arm were now re-established in sound activity, had shot and dressed the pigeons, gathered the fruits and vegetables, and did many other things, too numerous to mention, towards helping forward the day's great business, in which of course he, and the whole of Juan's family felt an immense personal interest.

Of course, there was an unlimited supply of whatever the homestead produced; but when the vegetables came on, there was among them an unexpected home dish of the whitest and mealiest of potatoes. I knew we had sweet potatoes and yuca which I had thought the next best thing to Irish potatoes, but here was the potato itself. I could not divine whence it came, for in making the chowder, I had been forced to substitute yuca for that indispensable vegetable, and I questioned Juanico about it the moment we left the table. For even Julio and Delfino did not recognize the stranger.

Tio explained by leading me to the corner of the yuca plat, and showing me a cluster of immense leaves, many of them more than a foot in diameter, He called this *yautilia*. I had found, growing among the weeds when I cleared up the old garden space, a few of these peculiar heart-shaped leaves, and asked

Juan what they were? He replied, with indifference, that "the roots were good enough to eat, when there were no plantains, no yuca, and no yams." On this very dubious recommendation, I concluded to give the plants a trial, and transplanted them in a double row where the hoe and weeder could attend to them while busy with the corn rows.

Cultivation had so much improved this neglected Indian *yautilia* that my friends did not recognize it, in the delicate and savory mash which was placed before them with the roasted fowls. For me I consider it a most valuable discovery.

I am persuaded that this root is capable of great improvement, and that it will be an exceedingly profitable crop when the ground is naturally favorable, and where thorough ploughing gives it fair play.

My first crop of corn is sold, and I have planted the ground with yuca and yautilia, in equal divisions. The bean ground, which is too full of stumps for ploughing, I am planting with sweet potatoes, and in December I shall probably be able to say which of the three is the most desirable as a money maker.

July is an excellent month for planting all of these, and the whole of the space left free by taking away the first crops of corn and beans is now, at the close of the month, green with thrifty successors of the root family.

CHAPTER IX.

AUGUST.

A drawback not altogether surprising.—A warning to new-comers. —How I paid for my experience.—Plantain walk.—Different varieties of bananas.—My *platanal*.—Industry of Juanico.—His brilliant strategy.—Felix Tisada.—Exhibit my improvements.—Amazement of the Dominican.—A proposal.—I take advantage of it.—Overwork myself.—Awake feverish and in pain.—Anita's advice.—Simple remedies.—Juanico and Felix wish to call a physician.—Each knows a worthy doctor.—They disagree.—Decide to employ neither.—My rapid recovery.—Valuable hints.

JUNE and July were exciting months. They were perhaps overcrowded with work. In fact I now feel that I swerved too often and too widely from the rule and moderation which I had strictly carried into all my labors in the earlier months of my residence here.

What with gathering in my first crop from the Home Field, and preparing the ground and planting the second crop, what with clearing the New Field, and building my dear and pleasant palenca cottage, I have lived and acted under the constant pressure of an unwise eagerness to do more than my means and strength warranted.

Yet after paying the penalty and counting the cost, there still remains a cheerful balance of satisfaction on my mind. When I step out in the bright and fragrant hour of sunrise, and see the blooming results of one poor man's work, in the teeming fields that speak of "something attempted, something *done*," I rejoice in my labors.

As I look abroad and sum up the bounteous freedom of a country life, I marvel at the patience with which I toiled in the treadmill routine of a city existence for so many weary years, always keenly anxious about the future, and never enjoying the calm certainty that even the doubtful tenure, by which I worked for daily bread, would hold good to the year's end.

Here at least, every week of well-applied labor gives fair promise of permanent reward. Every privation of the passing hour carries with it the balm of an abundant future recompense.

August is to a new beginner, in some respects, a more exacting month than July; for while it is particularly and prominently the time to set out his plantain walk, as well as to close the planting of his sweet potatoes, yuca and yautilia, there are three chances to one that his plan of labor may be broken in upon by a two or three hours' rain nearly every afternoon.

A new comer must avoid these drenching showers as he would an inevitable sentence to a week of chills and fever. One is almost sure to follow the other, if an unacclimated man is caught in a heavy rain while warm with work, unless he will take the trouble to seek immediate shelter, and put on dry clothes. For my own part, I was too careless on this point, and had to pay the price of my negligence.

I have been rashly impatient to finish planting the New Field this month, besides setting out a plantain walk around the south sweep of the winter garden, and more than once, while occupied by the double press of clearing the New Field and replanting the Home Lot, I had been caught in a sudden July shower without much regarding it. I was too intensely anxious to clear the way for my projects for August.

In addition to my previous plantings in May, June, and July, I have collected from my neighbors, and set out this month, more than a hundred plantains and banana roots—for I could not be content with less than the assurance of a full and never-failing supply of these precious tropical fruits—and it was a week's earnest labor for Juanico and myself to get them well in the ground.

Once fairly planted, in a proper manner, a plantain walk of two hundred roots becomes, with a very trifling amount of care, a standing fruit and vegetable supply for a large family.

The real plantain, boiled or roasted, serves in the place of bread in most of the country families. On many plantations the hands only have corn or cassava bread in the morning, and plantains at noon and night, and they generally prefer them to any other bread or vegetable. I cannot, therefore, expect to secure native laborers unless I provide a sure abundance of plantains in advance. There are several varieties of the plantain and banana, but the plantain proper being always eaten cooked, may be counted as a vegetable, while the luscious, melting banana ranks as a fruit. Both have the merit of being in season all the year. One variety, the *manzana* or "apple banana," a larger and hardier fruit than the delicate "fig banana," usually carried to the North, owes its name to the close resemblance in taste to a fine flavored apple when stewed or baked. When made into pies or dumplings, it is not easy to distinguish one from the other.

A fine plantain walk soon became a cherished feature in my homestead programme, and every step towards it was consequently made with careful forethought. A strip of rich, low land curved along the foot of the spring slope, beyond the moist ground occupied by my winter garden. This rich belt of low-lying interval placed about midway between the house site and the old cabin, and in full view of both, offers the most suitable soil and the most convenient position for a *platanal* to be found on the homestead, and from the first I have rejoiced over it as a precious advantage.

During May I began to prepare the ground fitly, to set out the roots as fast as I could manage to obtain them. I began by laying off the platanal for two hundred roots, though I had no idea when, where, or how I should get so many, for there is not one of my neighbors that has half the number—Don Julio excepted—and very few of them have any to spare on any terms. Nevertheless, with a devout trust in Providence, and some confidence in my own exertions to bring together the number and the varieties, which I consider necessary for a full and constant supply of the fruit for every week of the round year, I measured off my plantain walk, one hundred and fifty feet long by fifty feet wide. This is a fair allowance of space for eight rows of plants, twenty-five in a row and six feet apart.

While waiting for the plantain roots to come and take possession of their places, I put in a crop of the common quick-growing field bean of the country, but set stakes to mark where the plantains and bananas were to go, as fast as I should be able to procure them.

Down the centre of the Plantain Walk runs a broad aisle, nine feet in width, for the free passage of the donkey cart, and on each side of this central alley there is now a double row of plantains proper, one hundred in all, and to my eyes they make a goodly and refreshing show. Some of those planted in May are now gayly waving their immense leaves of vivid green, two yards long and a yard wide, eight feet above the soil. In three months more, I may hope to walk through a charming arcade of green banners the whole length of my plantain walk, but it will be well nigh a year before it can be said to be really in bearing.

After a good young platanal begins to yield fruit, the supply never flags in this luxuriant region. While one fruit-stalk is ripening its enormous cluster, others spring beside it to take its place at an early day; and so they keep up a perpetual succession of young shoots, of older stems just unfolding their great flower-cones of deep purple, and of eight or ten months old bearers, bending with long clusters of green and ripening fruit. Each original root becomes the centre of a cluster of plants in these different stages of ripeness, holding out through all seasons, from January to January, and never failing in a lifetime.

It required some patience and a trifle, perhaps somewhat more than a trifle, of persistent assurance to collect a sufficient stock of plantains to complete my coveted walk, but in one way and another the task was entirely accomplished by the middle of August.

The plantains proper were obtained with little difficulty, they being more abundant in the little gardens about Palenque and the Savana Grande, than bananas. When any of my neighbors came to buy, or as more frequently happened, to beg, a mess of nice vegetables, which they had been too idle or too careless to raise for themselves, I gave them more than they expected, but always with a Yankee hint that a few plantain roots would be an acceptable return for my ocra, chalots, tomatoes or limas, and these kindly people rarely came a second time without bringing the desired equivalent in the shape of a pair of plantain roots. In this way, and with the large contribution of some thirty roots from Don Julio's platanal, I had more than half of the double row of plantains each side of the central alley in the ground and already sending their broad, banner-like leaves a couple of feet above it, by the end of June. Outside the plantains proper, places were marked for a row of the manzana or "apple" banana, and again outside of these runs a finishing row on either hand of the melting "fig," which is of a lower growth and richer foliage than the others. The plantain has the inside place, because it runs up taller and does not rejoice in the full, untempered blaze of the sun so much as the sugary fig banana.

During all June, my faithful, unselfish man Friday, my poor, affectionate Juanico, made several forays into more distant settlements to obtain the complement of apple and fig bananas necessary to keep step with the plantains in our new Walk. He specially celebrated St. John's day by walking over to the town of Bani, fourteen miles, and there managed to inveigle an old friend of his into bringing over to me a donkey load of the much desired banana roots.

I was delighted to receive Juanico's friend Felix and his donkey load of fine *sipas*, though somewhat astonished at this prompt and brilliant success. I was not long, however, in discovering that Juanico had achieved this through his florid descriptions of our wonderful deeds in the farming line. In fact, he had even offered to teach his credulous friend the Yankee art and mystery of weeding corn, yuca, and other field crops with a donkey cultivator.

After Felix had assisted us to set out the banana roots, Juanico put Burro to the cultivator, and run through a few rows of corn of the last planting. The invigorating showers, and glowing sun of August had started a light crop of weeds, notwithstanding the thorough cleaning it had received in July, but the ground was mellow and as Burro walked along, this green growth of intruders vanished with magical celerity.

Felix was charmed with the performance of Burro and the weeding plough; so much so, that he begged permission to harness his own donkey, and work with him at cleaning all the corn in my home lot.

I graciously consented, and in one forenoon he did well and fully, the work usually assigned for a week's labor to first class native hands, but which none of them often perform.

This feat was a great delight to Felix, and the honest Bani farmer did not disguise the triumphant satisfaction which he promised himself in relating to his friends at home, that he had learned to do more work with one donkey and a little machine which he could carry about on his shoulder, than twelve of the best men in Bani could perform in the same time.

Following up this opening advantage, Juanico wrought up his friend's enthusiasm to a fever pitch by showing him the deep ploughing, and it culminated to overflowing at the sight of the sweeping rapidity of scythe work, when he cut the fodder for the donkey's night feed. Later in the day, Juanico walked with him through the planted avenues, which are now beautifully carpeted with thick grass, and give pleasant access to every part of the homestead, and explained why such pains had been taken to plant every thing in regular lines.

The Dominican was charmed with all he saw, and comprehended every thing very well, until Juanico spoke of the grafting process. He was naturally keen, and he understood at once that ploughs and cultivators must have a clear range, and that fruit-trees might perhaps pay for the trouble of trimming and weeding, but the absolute grafting of one variety of fruit on other stocks, seemed to him most extraordinary and a very doubtful experiment. "If such precious results were so easily obtained, why," he asked, "does not all the world have plenty of good fruit?" Common sense echoes, "Why, indeed?" Yet it is not in Santo Domingo alone that these things are treated as if they were not.

To convince him, we led the way to my thriving line of grafted oranges, and pointed to the still scarred and bandaged trees, which he could see, by the superior delicacy of the leaves, were really sweet orange scions, grafted on the hardy stocks of the sour native fruit. After much examination and an endless circle of questions, always beginning and ending with—"If this is really possible, why cannot I, Felix Tisada, also learn to graft fruit-trees?" he arrived at a firm conclusion that he had a genius for the American system of cultivation, and proposed to become my disciple, something after the fashion of my dear and noble friend Delfino. I accepted the offer to a certain degree, but I could not but feel the vast difference between *him* and Felix Tisada. One is an instructed gentleman, with a soul as bright as the sun and as open as the day, with a spirit that lighted up the hardest toil; while the other is simply an unlettered laborer of Bani, used to work, and willing to do it, but who can bring no luxury of companionship to enliven labor or rest.

Yet the proposition of Felix was not one to be lightly rejected by a man in my circumstances. He wanted to learn the use of the heavy ox-plough, and also to acquire the art of grafting, and said he was ready to accommodate himself to any terms I chose to name that would secure these objects. Juanico delivered me the message after the two had talked the matter well over between themselves, and he manifested so much interest in it, that I accepted the bargain almost exactly as he stated it. Felix was to come over about the middle of August, with his own yoke of oxen, and plough up all the land I might have ready for the purpose, and assist me in planting the field with corn and potatoes. I agreed, on my part, that Juanico and the light plough should be turned into his cotton field for as many days in September as he should work in my field in August—that is, in planting it, for the ploughing work counted for nothing, as it was done in the way of instruction.

Felix was eager to buy or borrow the heavy ox-plough for a few weeks, to break up the ground for a fall planting of corn, generally the most profitable corn crop of the year, but I could not oblige him in that point.

The plough was already sold, and at a liberal price, to Don Julio, and I had only the right to use it for my own work during the current year. As yet, there is no other ox-plough in this region, though I have ordered out three large ploughs, of the very best construction, for myself and friends, but we cannot expect to receive them before November, and by that time the dry season will be too close upon us for any more ploughing and planting this winter. As for the grafting lessons, I was dubious about their successful outcome at that season; but to teach him the form of operation, I willingly devoted an hour in the afternoon in setting a dozen slips from a large, sweet-fruited guava, on a handsome tree, very prettily situated near the cottage, but which bears a small, sour fruit. If any of them should *take*, it would be a most encouraging precedent; if not, the loss was nothing to alarm me.

This grafting dates back to the last week in June, when Felix came with his first load of banana-roots; and in the press of our July planting and building, the guava grafts were entirely neglected by me, although Juanico, as I afterwards learned, had kept an eye of attentive curiosity on the results. He had exacted from Felix the promise to bring another load of bananas when he returned to us to practise with the ox-plough, and my honest Juanico felt himself, as it were, pledged to produce the guava graftings in a state of healthy growth. I had given no such assurance, for I much doubted the possibility of scions taking in the full tide of sap, and fruit-bearing; but nothing seems impossible in this generous climate. Seven—more than half of the scions—appear to have "set." At any rate they are green with new leaves, to the unbounded admiration of Felix, and not a little, I must confess it, to my own astonishment.

I had but very moderate confidence in the punctuality of Felix, and was occupied with my plantain walk, hoeing up the weedy grass, and heaping it in little hills between but not too close upon the plants, thinking over the feasibility of making an excursion to Bani in search of roots enough to fill out my rows, for I had exhausted the spare *hijos*—young sprouts—of my neighbors, when my reflections were arrested by the clamorous driving of oxen on our new road. They came near, stopped at the gate, passed through it. Could it, perchance, be Felix, after all? Has he really committed the rare and most un-Dominican act of keeping his engagement to the day and letter? I stepped forward to assure myself of the truth, and, sure enough, I met him tearing down the slope, mounted on one ox and leading another by a long rope attached to the nostril.

"*Aqui estamos Señor.*" "Here we are, I and the oxen, and the bananas," shouted Felix, on catching sight of me—"Here we are, at your orders. Your friends and servants—all three of us," he added, sliding down from his extraordinary perch on, or among, a huge pile of roots, and affectionately patting the patient animal as he spoke.

An American would have scouted the idea of piling such a quantity of stuff on the backs of a pair of oxen, and then riding and driving them fourteen miles at a quick step, that is quick for horned steeds, but nothing of the kind daunts a genuine child of this island.

While I was uttering a few words of welcome, Felix unloosed divers cords, and down dropped the capacious folds of native matting, and with them rolled out a welcome supply of bananas, sufficient to complete my plantain walk, and have a few roots of "figs" for Anita, who had earnestly bespoke the first sprouts I could spare, for her cottage door. In the afternoon we had several passing showers, but I was in such haste to plant my *sepas* that in spite of the wet I worked on, and Juanico and Felix assisted until the last one was set, and my Plantain Walk completely filled out. I went to sleep that night with the comforting conviction that my homestead now contains an ample and established orchard of the most necessary and valuable of tropical fruits.

In the morning I felt heavy and feverish for the first time since my arrival in Santo Domingo. I had no taste for my breakfast or my work, and I ached to return to my cot for another hour's rest, but Felix and his oxen were waiting on me, and I forced myself to the task of seeing them well started with the plough. Juanico, who had already learned something of this kind of work, entreated me to return home, and leave him and Felix to go on with the ploughing; but the effort and excitement of teaching such a willing and anxious pupil as Felix, kept me up an hour or two longer. At last a dizzy headache and a succession of slight chills warned me that I could no longer resist the approaching fever.

Long before my regular hour of eleven, I was obliged to resign the charge of the plough in favor of Juanico, and seek the shelter of the palenca. I met Anita at the spring, getting water, and asked her to give me a drink. She looked up in surprise, and said in tones of concern, that I had "the strangers' fever." "Why do you think so, Anita?" I feebly inquired. She replied that she saw it in my heavy eyes and "yellow paleness." There was a disagreeable ring in the words "*strangers'* fever and "yellow paleness," to ears that, from childhood up, have been filled with dreadful stories of the havoc of tropical fevers. Many people at the North fancy that half the families that emigrate to the tropics are certain to die off directly with yellow fever, or black vomit, or some other terrible malady; and, notwithstanding that I personally knew scores of emigrants who had passed the ordeal of a change of climate without a day's serious illness, these old ideas weighed heavily on me.

A depressing return of my youthful horror of yellow fever swept across me, as I laid my throbbing head on the pillow, yet I thought of medicine with a loathing distrust. The nearest doctor was four miles off, somewhere on the River Nizao, and I was not inclined to send for him, any way. I have no passion for swallowing apothecaries' shops, either in hap-hazard experiments or according to learned rules. So I told Anita she must cure me by good nursing, and asked her to make me a cooling drink of ripe limes. She, however, insisted on making me, first of all, a warm "*tisana*" of *green* limes, to drive out the chills.

This is the simple, and generally successful, remedy of the country. These people never think of calling a physician for a common fever. Half a dozen green limes, not fully grown, are cut up in a pitcher of boiling water, which is well covered until it is so far cooled that the patient can drink it without inconvenience. It is sweetened to one's taste, and I found it extremely acceptable, even hot, at least while the creeping chills had possession of my aching frame. As they passed off and a scorching fever took their place, the cooled tisana was, if possible, still more agreeable to my parched tongue, and I drank of it without stint.

Felix and Juanico came in to see me at noon, and both of them expressed a great desire to have a doctor called. The *remedios* of the country were well enough for the poor natives, they said, but not for me, a stranger accustomed to precious medicines, to medicines worth their weight in gold. For me, mere *tisanas* were declared to be altogether too simple, and, of course, were out of question. They considered that nothing short of a regular doctor had a right to cure me. On *a* doctor, therefore, they were fully agreed, but on *the* doctor to be intrusted with my case, there arose a formidable difference of opinion. Juanico had unlimited faith in a certain somebody, whom he declared to be an "angel of science"—the Dominicans are rich in splendid phrases—but Felix said this medical wonder was terribly unlucky with his patients, and wanted to start off, to I know not what distant region, for another physician who was a "well of experience." Juanico stoutly objected to this "Well of Experience" as much more unlucky with his patients than his own "Angel of Science."

Between them I determined not to try either, and I ended the discussion by telling them both that I would trust to *tisanas* and cold water for that day and the next, and after that we would think about a doctor, if by that time the fever did not abate.

That night was indeed a night of distress. Racking pains in my head, back, and limbs, banished sleep, and I tossed in restless anguish through the long, long night, hopeless of rest and praying for daylight. Anita went home at dark, leaving me a pitcher of fresh lemonade within reach, and charging Juanico to keep bathing my head with cool water. It was not necessary to charge Juanico to take good care of me, for he was not willing to leave me for a moment. I begged him to go to his own cot in the old cabin, where Felix had slung his hammock, and get his usual sleep, in order to assist at the plough in the morning, but he plead so earnestly for the privilege of bringing in his blanket and lying down at the foot of my bed, that it was easier to submit to his wishes than to resist his affectionate importunity.

In the gray of the morning I fell asleep for an hour, and when I opened my eyes I saw Juanico staggering up the path under a back-load of cocoa-nuts. He had slipped away before daylight and walked over to Don Julio's "for advice and water cocoa-nuts to cure my fever." He came back with both. Don Julio was not at home, but his experienced Mayoral sent me his "advice" to persevere with *tisanas* of lime and sour orange, while the *warm* chills were upon me as well as during the copious perspirations, which he said I must expect, for three days at least, close upon the fever that would follow the chills. In the quiet intervals I was to be freely indulged in the cool, transparent water of green cocoa-nuts. If I felt any desire to eat in these intervals, which it happened I did not, then I might be allowed the water of a ripe cocoa-nut, as a nourishment. This was all the medical advice I received, and these agreeable beverages were literally and strictly all the medicine I have taken for my acclimating fever. The yellow fever is unknown in this section of the Island of Santo Domingo and the "strangers' fever" is, to my mind, simply a milder type of the too common "chills and fever" of the Western States of the Union.

Judging from my own experience, and from the statements of my friends, I should say that the acclimating "ague and fever" of the Upper Mississippi, takes a much longer hold and is in every way more malignant in character than the Dominican *calentura.* That seldom runs more than nine days, and frequently not more than three, if the patient turns at once to a cooling *tisana*, and will abstain from gross food during the intervals between the fever chills. The first day or two of dizzy headache, and pains in the back and limbs—the premonitory symptoms—are so much alike in almost every case, that a new settler can understand at once the nature of the attack, and can treat it for himself with confidence.

I had three very sick days, but after they had passed I walked out every morning to see how Felix and Juanico were succeeding with the plough. Taking an hour under the nearest shade-tree, I would creep back to my diet broths, and rest on my cot until the afternoon. I lost but three consecutive days in which I was confined to the cottage; after them, on alternate days, I had three afternoons of slight chills, with decreasing fever on each occasion, but with some headaches and a general sense of debility throughout most of the day. Between these sick days, there regularly intervened days of comparative health, as in the chills and fever of the West, and in those days I went out for a longer stay in the field, and inhaled, with unspeakable zest, the cool, invigorating freshness of the morning.

I felt able and anxious to lend a hand to the farming work in those mornings, but I refrained, as my experienced friend Don Julio, who came over every day to see me, after he returned from the city, impressed upon me the prudence of carefully nursing back my lost strength, instead of exhausting the little stock on hand by premature exertions.

In nine days I was very nearly myself again; but, in the mean time, August had almost slipped away, and much of my August planting will run into September. Felix staid with me a fortnight, and he and Juanico have done far better than I could have hoped from such unpractised hands. The corn they planted already stands out in green, well defined rows, with plenty of squashes and calabasitas springing up between them. The potatoes look thrifty and promising for the December and January market. My plantain walk has started beautifully, and the homestead has not suffered during my illness, every thing considered. The bounties and blessings of August have been manifold, and even its sick-bed lessons are precious in their teachings.

CHAPTER X.

SEPTEMBER.

Famous yield of sweet potatoes.—Contract with Captain Ramirez.—The Captain becomes alarmed.—His fears quieted.—Anita's transactions with the natives.—Cocoa-nut grove.—Its importance.—Am in great perplexity.—Juanico plays the *diplomat.*—Felix comes to my relief.—An amusing scene.—A friendly contest.—Sale of the "cultivator."—What Felix undertakes.—How Felix is swindled.—My despair.—A fresh comer in the scene.—Arrival of Rosa Dalmeyda.—Her mission.—How we arrange matters.—Success at last.

THREE days of acclimating fever, and six more of forced idleness for the restoration of my strength, broke somewhat into my plans and labors for August, but this bright and bountiful September has set things square again.

The week of slow recovery was favorable to a thoughtful review of what had been done, and what left undone, in the past seven months of active labor, and this led to one or two material changes in the arrangements for the future months of the year.

In the Home Field, containing rather more than eight acres within the new fence, I have now in full bearing nearly every tropical fruit, and all the vegetables known in northern markets, with the exception of peas and Irish potatoes; besides many kinds that are very scarce, if not unknown, in Europe and the United States.

By selecting a piece of wet ground below the spring, and planting it from seedling beds made in January, and watered during February and a part of March, I had secured such a large and varied supply of vegetables for the dry season, that the sale of my surplus abundance—strictly the produce of my own labor—has been more than sufficient to pay the hire of three men in clearing and fencing the new field of twenty acres. The satin-wood, *campeche*, and mahogany cut from this new field have completely paid for my homestead, besides covering the expense of closing in and roofing over my cottage.

My half an acre, more or less, of moist, fertile soil;

my Winter Garden, as I love to call it, because it is my reliance for food and profit in the dry season between the first of January and the middle of March; has cost me about as much hard work to get it well under way as the other four and a half or five acres planted with corn, beans, yuca, and sweet potatoes. But then it has returned me profits in proportion. Indeed, the sum total of results has been a delightful astonishment to me, and would be incredible to a farmer accustomed to the dead loss of the frosty season in cold climates.

The yield of sweet potatoes was so abundant, in consequence of ploughing the ground previous to planting instead of scratching it over with the hoe, and of my regularly cleaning them *twice* with the donkey cultivator instead of *once* half-scraping away the weeds here and there, that the whole neighborhood has crowded upon me in mass to wonder at it. It is not only the most plentiful crop, and of the largest potatoes ever seen, but it is a month earlier than any of theirs, and comes into market in season to command the highest prices.

Next year, if I live, I shall try to be yet another month earlier, with a still better crop. The clean and mellow soil invited the sun and rain to feed the growing bulbs generously with warmth and moisture, and, like well-fed children, they have proved their good keeping by their round and healthy plumpness.

Half of the neighborhood flocked to see the "American method" of digging potatoes; and when the number of curious visitors began to be troublesome, I set them, one and all, picking from the furrows as I laid the potatoes open with the mule plough. The incurable idlers speedily vanished, but those who remained, with a wish to be useful, I took care to pay, by giving them a portion of what they gathered. Some of them came back the second, and even the third day, and at the close of the ingathering many carried home more than they are likely to get from their own ill-kept gardens.

This September crop leaves the ground free for a replanting, either with potatoes for the latter part of winter and early spring market, or with corn and *calabasitas* for sale in all December. One or the other is what a Dominican farmer would do, and it had been my intention to follow the native custom, but on reflection I concluded to plant it with *yautilia*, the nearest thing possible to a white and mealy Irish potato. I must wait longer for the returns, as this excellent root does not mature in less than seven months; but when it is ripe and ready it yields surprisingly, and will always command one dollar a bushel.

By the way, I must not forget to note that Captain Ramirez contracted with me to take, at the Palenque Landing, all the sweet potatoes that I could deliver to him before the 20th of September, at one dollar the bushel.

To meet this engagement, I went into the field on Monday, the 8th of September, with a lot of lads whom I hired to pick up as I ploughed out the potatoes, and Juanico followed with his donkey cart, to take them down to the landing, and put them on board the boat bound for Santo Domingo city, in the evening. At four in the afternoon the little

Alice had received all she had room for, in addition to her other cargo; but Capt. Ramirez contrived a tent, out of a couple of old sails, to shelter the balance, and have it ready to ship on his return trip.

It rained late in the day, and again in the afternoons of the two succeeding days, but we had bright, clear forenoons, and we made the most of them. When the Alice returned on Thursday, and brought up close to the tent, her good captain was startled to find his extemporized storehouse filled to overflowing with potatoes.

"Where did all these come from?" he asked, almost in dismay. "I never saw such a quantity of potatoes in one heap since I have lived on this island."

There appeared to be more than there really were, and Juanico, who had just brought in another load, assured him there were not quite one hundred bushels in the pile, all told. Ramirez thought there must be much more, and was really uneasy about the possibility of selling such a quantity all in one week. For in such a petty peddling way is the city of Santo Domingo, a town of about 12,000 inhabitants, supplied with its every-day demands in this line, that an experienced purveyor like Ramirez was seriously afraid of overstocking the market by offering one hundred bushels of potatoes at once! He told me so quite seriously, when he ran up for half an hour in the evening, to settle our last month's garden account and talk over his fears.

I laughed him out of them directly, but to set his mind fully at rest, I proposed to relieve him of his contract for the remainder of my potato crop, if the portion of it already at the landing should not sell to advantage. He had sold forty bushels, the first delivery from his boat, almost as soon as he made fast to the river bank at Santo Domingo city, and I had no doubt that the fine size and quality of that instalment would create a demand for the rest.

So it turned out. It was rather early in the season for abundant supplies, and when the Alice again rounded into the lovely bay, Saturday night, Captain Ramirez rushed up to the cottage, after ten o'clock, to beg of me to have another hundred bushels ready for him early in the week, as he had engaged that amount among the Dominican retailers, provided they were immediately forthcoming, while prices were lively.

I was prepared for this, and the additional quantity was punctually delivered in season for shipment during the week, for I was quite as anxious to clear the field for my *yautilia* planting, not to mention the interesting feature of dollars, as Ramirez was to catch the high tide of the market.

Before the twentieth, every potato not reserved for my own use was disposed of, and the cash as good as in hand.

My first yuca crop in the Home Field will be the next in order, and it will probably net me about as much as the corn and potatoes have already done. The beans, green and ripe, have defrayed almost entirely the table expenses of my frugal housekeeping. Anita and her children have traded quite on their own responsibility, for me and for themselves, with the whole circle of their acquaintance, for eggs, chickens, cassava bread, and fresh fish; and I have never heard of any other current coin in their transactions than these beans, except perhaps a few tomatoes, or a handful of bird-pepper thrown in to make change.

Luxuries I have not aspired to; but the daily wants, and even the simple comforts, of a plain country life have never been wanting, no, not for a single day, though oftentimes they have come, I scarcely know how, like the needful showers or the silent refreshing dew, from the overflowing kindness of my Heavenly Father.

Having now the means in hand to employ help, I directed Juanico to find a couple of good men to assist him in preparing the ground and planting the *yautilia*, for there was hardly time to finish the work belonging to this month. Besides this, I wanted every hour I could possibly command for a new enterprise of my own; an enterprise I now consider of no slight importance, though it had hitherto escaped my attention.

In common with the majority of Dominicans, as well as strangers, I had never duly weighed the importance, I may say the indispensable necessity to a farmer, of a *cocoa-nut grove.*

But its value was brought home to me in the acclimating fever of August. Then, when my aching frame was stretched on a sick-bed, and my whole system was parched with fever, the cool and wholesome water of the cocoa-nut was like purest nectar to my burning palate. The milk, expressed through the grated meat of the ripe nut, is a delicate substitute for both milk and eggs in coffee, custards, and many other little comforts of the country. The fresh oil, if really fresh, and made with care and neatness, is held by competent cooks as fully equal to butter and olive oil in dressing salads and vegetables. When it is too old for the table or for medicine, it is excellent fuel for lamps. As a medicine, it has all the merits of castor-oil with none of its bad after consequences, besides being free from its disgusting nauseousness. In addition to all these good qualities, the limpid and almost tasteless oil of cocoa-nuts is of itself an excellent liniment for bruised or rheumatic limbs. I am told that the Indians in Central America use it constantly, internally and externally, as a panacea for all affections of the lungs and chest, and I have myself seen enough of its healing effects to hold it in most sincere respect. Yet with all this, while I had labored to gather almost every other useful fruit within the compass of my small homestead, I had by some strange oversight made no calculation whatever about planting a cocoa-nut grove.

I should have attended to this in July, August, or September, for in those rainy months, as I now learn, the young roots strike well into the soil, and get such a deep hold, that in the drier after months and years they defy the drought and continue to shoot up vigorously, with very slight regard to wet or dry seasons. To lose September, was to run the risk of losing half a year's growth of the sprouted cocoa-nuts, in case October happens to be a dry month; yet I saw no time to plant them, for I could not think of failing in my engagement to send Juanico and my mule plough to Bani, before the close of September, to assist Felix in cleaning his cotton field.

Felix himself came to relieve me from this per plexity. Whether or not he received beforehand a hint to that purpose, from my quiet but never inattentive Juanico, I cannot say, for we have never had a word on the subject. I have a private surmise; but all I know is that it so fell out, when I sent over my incomparable man Friday to inquire at what time Felix would require our help, that he returned with Felix himself, both of them brimming over with a new set of propositions.

Felix wanted to buy either the donkey cultivator or the mule plough, he was not particular which, but rather preferred the "cultivator." He said he did not wish to order one from the United States, for something imperfect might come, or at least some *máquina* which he did not understand. He esteemed mine because he had tried both plough and weeder, and knew them to be "miracles of utility." Therefore he would "supplicate" me to hear the explanations he had made to his friend Juanico, who, he observed, in an emphatic parenthesis, was my attached and faithful servant, like himself, and when I should understand the whole business, he hoped and believed that I would render him the favor he so ardently solicited.

After such a splendid harangue, I could only say in a few words that I had not dreamed of parting with either plough or cultivator, seeing there were no others in Santo Domingo, but that I would with much pleasure write to the United States and obtain precisely similar articles for him, in the course of perhaps two months.

"But have the kindness to hear from Juanico the explanations which I have had with him on this affair before you give me a positive answer," said Felix.

"Cannot you state them for yourself, Felix?" I asked, somewhat amused at the idea of his employing another to speak for him when he was there present, and capable at any time, and on any subject, of out-talking half a dozen Juanicos.

"Excuse me, Señor. Juanico can express it all in the most proper manner," said Felix, bowing and backing himself out of the door, leaving the hitherto silent Juanico in sole possession of the floor.

"Well, Juanico, what does our friend Felix expect of me?" I inquired. Juanico came to the point at a bound. He is not the man to waste time in circumlocution.

"Felix is crazy to own a plough, and he will contract to plant and guarantee the success of fifty *cocoas nacidos* (sprouted cocoa-nuts) as a premium on the regular price, which he will pay in money."

"How did he happen to think of the cocoa-nut planting?" I asked, a little mischievously, for these the footprints of Juanico's diplomacy were too plain to require all the "explanations" with which Felix covered himself as with a mantle of state.

"You were speaking of a cocoa-nut grove, Señor," said Juanico, modestly, "and Felix knows better than any one else around here, not only where to look for the sprouted nuts, but also how to plant them properly. It is not every one who has a lucky hand in planting cocoa-nuts," he added, softly.

"His offer is a tempting one, Juanico, but I fear it is growing rather late for planting this year. We owe Felix plough-work for all next week, and after that we must think of getting in our early yuca, to meet our engagement with Captain Ramirez. This will carry us so far into October, that I am afraid to undertake the cocoa-nut grove this fall."

"If it is your will to plant one, Señor, Felix must set aside his work until yours is done. All that is perfectly understood," said Juanico, with a smile of gentle satisfaction.

"But then comes our own fall work," I continued, dubiously. "How are we to manage the crops in the new field, Juanico, without at least one ploughing? We must turn under the first heavy crop of weeds, and go over it once, if not twice, with the cultivator."

"That is understood also, Señor, if you please to have it so," answered Juanico, quietly, in the tone of one who has thoroughly explored a knotty question, and feels that he has mastered all its rough points. "Felix will be satisfied to have me and the plough for a week in October. He will not ask for it until after the cocoa-nut grove is arranged to your complete satisfaction. At the end of the week

Juanico and the plough will return to you, Señor, if it please God, in a disposition to serve you until you have no more need of them."

"It will be a long time before the day comes when I shall not need you, my faithful Juanico," I answered in hearty sincerity; "but as to the plough, it would seem that your plan is to sell it to Felix, but keep it for my own use all the same."

Juanico smiled the soft, winning smile that becomes so well his handsome mouth and dark Indian face, but made no other reply.

"I think Felix has set his mind more on the donkey cultivator than on the mule plough," I resumed, after reflecting a moment.

"He will be well contented with either one of them," said Juanico in reply; "but whichever *máquina* you may choose to grant him, he receives on the condition "that it must remain at your command while you have use for it."

"On these conditions, Juanico, I think we may afford to part with the cultivator as soon as we have given the October cleaning to our new crops. Felix, it seems, pays for it in advance, and has the temporary use of it when we can spare it, and only receives it finally, late in the fall, when we have no further need for it, and when consequently it cannot serve him for this year's work. It strikes me, Juanico, that this is a safe bargain, on our side at least."

"Then you are satisfied with my explanation, Señor!" said Juanico, with unwonted animation. "Felix may count on having one of the *máquinas*."

"Yes, if he seriously desires it on such terms," I replied. "But will he commence planting my cocoa-nut grove without delay?"

"Ah, Señor, you may be certain of it. He will plunder his own mother if there is no other way to get fifty sprouted nuts, and will have them here and planted within three days." said Juanico, confidently.

Still, with the most enthusiastic desire to perfect the bargain at the quickest, Felix had not only to exert himself with energy, but I had to work with him, and engage another man to work with us, to get through the business in a week.

There was some hesitation in the choice of a part of the ground. The cocoa-nut delights in a sandy and not too rich soil, where its extensive roots can strike deep and spread far; and the only suitable place is at the farther side of the new field, more out of sight than I like to place a tempting fruit-grove. The ground had been cleared with reference to an October planting of pole-beans, and the tall stems of a thicket of saplings had been purposely left for the accommodation of the climbing vines We had to cut these bean-supports away in a great measure, to make room for the cocoa-nuts in their due spaces, twenty-five feet apart; and, when we came to measure the ground, it appeared there was not enough of this sandy hollow under fence to accommodate more than forty trees. On the other side of the new field fence, in the ten or twelve acres still unenclosed, which I reserve for pasture, there is a larger strip of sandy soil, running the whole breadth of the "outside land," along the road, but it is not safe in its present unenclosed condition.

The animals at large would browse off the young

leaves and kill the plants, if any were set out before it was fenced, and more fencing is out of question this year; so I had to take things as they were.

One whole day was spent in clearing the lines, and the second I left my hired hand to dig the holes where I had marked places for them, and went home to send Juanico down to the beach for a cart-load of salt sea-sand.

While at the cottage Felix arrived with a very long face, and a very short account of sprouted cocoa-nuts. He had ranged from Savana Grande to Bani and had obtained only fourteen reliable nuts. "There is a miserable wretch at Bani," he said, with a bitterness almost comical in its concentration, "who had more than three dozen laid up in a corner of his plantain walk. Only last night he exchanged all these with me for a sheep, which I delivered to him on the spot, but now the false dog refuses to complete his bargain, and I had to almost take with violence, from one friend and another, these few I have brought you."

"Well, Felix, we will go out and plant these to-day. To-morrow we may find more in some other quarter."

Felix shook his head dolefully, as much as to say that it was a desperate hope, and that when *he* despaired of accomplishing any thing it was folly for any other man to think of succeeding. He followed me to the field with his meagre donkey-load nevertheless, and before we had finished our planting he had talked himself into a more cheerful view of the case. It was an alleviating circumstance that, for want of immediate space, probably no more than forty *nacidos* would be required this year. I am obstinate in the idea, that it is not profitable to plant fruit-trees of any kind in a crowded, irregular manner, still less would I waste time and trouble in setting them out in an unsafe situation, where the chances are strongly against their living six months. After all, a grove of forty bearing trees will yield a goodly supply of cocoa-nuts.

In a congenial soil, and with ample space, a cocoa will drop about two hundred nuts in a year, while in a clayey or rocky soil a crowded grove will scarcely average forty. When treated two or three times a year to a handful of salt, by throwing it into the green heart of the plume of branches, a thriving cocoa will often begin to bear in five years ; but without this attention it is not to be expected under its seventh year,—a gain of two years in time and a double yield of fruit for a half hour of attention, and perhaps a pint of salt to each tree.

In planting, it is only necessary to dig a hole somewhat more than large enough to hold the sprouted nut, which will generally have a little rootlet or two piercing through the husk, at the same time that a green tuft emerges from the stem end. Two or three quarts of moist sea-sand is thrown under and around the nut, when the sea-sand is obtainable ; and when it is not, a handful of common salt is mixed with the earth and put in lightly around it in place of the sand. The nut should be set with just enough pressure to hold the sprout upright in its place, with the upper surface of the nut at the level or slightly above the level of the ground, and if it can be shaded for a month or two it is all the better.

The Dominicans call this *very* careful planting, and this, with the moderate trouble of hoeing away the weeds three or four times the first year—about as much labor as a Northern farmer bestows upon every hill of corn which he raises—is positively all that the neatest and most considerate of planters ever thinks of devoting to a cocoa-nut grove. With this much care, not one out of twenty healthy sprouts will fail to flourish, if planted any time between the beginning of May and the last of September. Yet many, if not most, of the small land owners on this island consent to live without the comfort of possessing a single one of these precious and hardy trees on their homesteads.

I shall try hard to procure forty nuts at least, since I cannot carry out my plan for fifty, and am not likely to be disappointed in their well-being.

Felix and I had planted our first fourteen, and were helping Juanico distribute his load of sea-sand in the holes my hired man was making for their companions, should I have the good fortune to obtain them, when the gathering clouds warned us to seek shelter from a heavy rain not far off.

Felix started on a run directly for the cottage, and Juanico and I followed with the donkey-cart by the road, after finishing with the sand. As we were opening the gate of the Home Field, Juanico happened to glance down the road, and spied a woman travelling at extraordinary speed, considering that she was mounted on a wonderfully small donkey, for, as a rule, none of these animals are remarkable for swiftness. She called out to us, to ask if there was not a gentleman known as Señor Vecino who lived somewhere in this neighborhood. I replied that I answered to that name among my neighbors, and waited for her to draw up and take breath, although the sky was rapidly darkening overhead.

"If you are the Señor, I am your servant Rosa Dalmeyda, and have some business with you," she said, as she joined us.

"In that case I must beg of you to proceed to the house, for the rain will be upon us in a moment," I answered, wondering what she could want of me, and how I should dispose of her this rainy evening.

I hastened to conduct my unexpected visitor to the cottage; and we were not a second too soon, for the thunder-storm burst upon us in torrents before we were fairly seated. Felix had gone, for the moment, to the old cabin, where he has his night-quarters, and Juanico hurried to the shed behind it, to shelter Burro and the stranger's donkey, so that I was left alone to attend to my visitor, and learn at her pleasure what business she had come to transact with me. I was not kept long in suspense.

The amiable Rosa informed me off-hand that she was the wife of "the man Andres, who had sold a quantity of magnificent *cocoas nacidas* to 'Señor' Felix," which magnificent *nacidas* she understood were destined for me; and she had made this journey to know if in truth I wanted to buy them, and whether I was disposed to pay for them in silver.

I answered by asking if her husband had not already received from "Señor" Felix the payment agreed upon. With a charming frankness Rosa

Dalmeyda admitted that the "man Andres" had, only the night before, received a young sheep according to contract; further, that he had brought it home and killed it, but that he had carried off most of the meat and sold it for rum.

"Andres went to bed drunk," she continued, "and I went out with my son and nephew and hid the *nacidas* where the beast could not find them in the morning." Rosa then went on to inform me, in the free and easy spirit of frankness characteristic of her class, that for me there would be no cocoa-nuts until she saw the silver.

"So Señor Felix cannot receive the cocoa-nuts he has paid for, and I perhaps may not obtain them at all?" I observed, interrogatively.

"Of course not, Señor, unless I am paid for them," said Rosa, with a determined toss of her head. "It is I who own the trees. *I* planted them when we were first married, and *I* must have the price for the nuts."

"But Señor Felix may choose to call Andres before the Alcalde for selling property that does not belong to him," I ventured to observe; "and this you know, Rosa, is a matter of imprisonment under the Spanish law."

"That is not my affair," replied the affectionate wife, with sublime composure. "What concerns *me* is, to learn whether you decide to buy my cocoa-nuts. Yes or no?"

"That depends upon what Felix says, and there he is to give us his opinion on the subject," I said, looking up at Felix, who had stopped in the doorway, surprised at this sudden apparition of his Bani neighbor in my premises.

Felix was severely polite with her, but she forced him, in spite of every thing, to admit that she was really the owner of the cocoa-nuts, and that she had, by law and custom, the right to receive payment for them. Felix protested against paying twice, but I finally compromised matters by agreeing to give her *un real de diez* each—ten cents—for twenty-six nuts, the number I then thought I required to fill out my space.

As soon as this was settled Rosa asked for her

donkey, for the shower was over, and started off by the starlight to meet her nephew at the house of a friend in the neighborhood. She had out-rode the boy because his donkey was loaded with a portion of the very *nacidas* in question, which she now declared she had brought with her, in the faith that I must and would buy them, as there were no others to be had at that moment. She promised, and she kept her promise, to be at the gate of the new field with her whole load punctually at sunrise. She also engaged that her nephew should assist in planting them, and that too was fulfilled to the letter.

At break of day Juanico started for the beach for another load of sea-sand, while Felix and I, after an early cup of coffee, went directly to the field to meet Rosa and her charge. Many hands make light work, and the balance of my triple row of sprouted cocoas were in the ground by ten in the forenoon. We added one more plant to our first line of fourteen, making fifteen in the row nearest the fence, and set twelve in each of the two parallel rows, and then the nuts gave out.

On close measuring, I saw that by removing two large stumps, which were badly in the way, I could extend the second and third lines as far as the first, and so make my cocoa-grove a regular oblong of two hundred and seventy-five feet by seventy-five, containing three lines of cocoas—fifteen in each line and forty-five in all. This will entirely fill up the only bit of poor land I have under fence, and will scarcely trench on the good land by it. Before we left the field I made my arrangements to have the stumps dug out, and secured another half dozen *nacidas* from Rosa.

She was punctual, and to-day, the 29th of September, the planting of my cocoa-nut grove is, happily for me, an accomplished fact.

CHAPTER XI.

OCTOBER.

Triumph of Felix.—Auspicious return of Juanico.—His unwonted gayety.—How accounted for.—Don Delfino imports a Stump-Extractor.—Great excitement in the neighborhood.—We muster our forces.—How we obtain recruits.—The process of stump-extracting.—Anita's collation.—Private dinner in the North Arbor.—Don Julio appears again.—Fresh attack on the enemy.—Close of the contest.—The "Extractor" victorious.—Delfino's invitation.—I accept it.—His plantation.—What we do there.

THIS lovely October has been almost a month of festival, though by no means a month of idleness. At the close of September Felix carried off in triumph the mule-plough and the donkey-cultivator, together with Juanico to aid in their management, and he astonished to his heart's content the good people of Bani by their stupendous success in the cotton-field.

This field, of perhaps three acres in extent, had

been prepared and planted by the hoe alone in all May, and it is now bursting into ripe and snowy bolls in every direction. It was while Felix was giving this field its first clearing with the hoe, that he heard from some stray visitor an account of the wonderful performances of the donkey "limpiador" in my corn-field, and he forthwith formed a desire to see its action, but with scarcely the remotest idea of ever owning one himself.

When Juanico, his cousin three times removed, applied to him for banana-roots, I presume the hope and the way of using such *máquinas* himself first opened dimly before him, and he pursued the thought until he has realized his desire.

In a week Juanico, Felix, and the *máquinas* had among them done all that it was possible to do for his corn and cotton-fields, both being, in fact, many weeks past the time in which the weeding ought to have been performed; but the profound ambition of Felix was perfectly accomplished. He overwhelmed the doubts of his hitherto incredulous and sneering neighbors by his splendid operations, and, in his own words, "granting that it was attempted somewhat late in the season, it was worth more than it cost to tear up the ground so magnificently."

The whole turn-out came back radiant with victory. Felix, Juanico, the donkey-cart, with plough and cultivator stowed safe and sound amid a pile of cabbages and sugar-cane, rolled up to the cottage—the whole concern singing and rattling in a chorus of glee—very late Saturday night. They found me still up, and as happy as themselves.

Delfino had rode in an hour before them, and had promised to stay most of the coming week with me. He expected by the Alice some farming implements, which had just arrived at Santo Domingo City in a vessel from New York, and we were to examine and prove some of them at my place before they were sent up to his plantation.

Juanico was delighted to see his old master, and imputed his unwonted flow of gayety, which he declared he had felt all the way home from Bani, "to an inspiration that a great pleasure was awaiting him." I was so uncharitable as to suspect that a drop or two of native spirits had some part in unloosing the tongue of my usually serious and quiet retainer, but I kept this unfeeling suspicion closely to myself.

Felix had only returned with Juanico to spend Sunday and attend church at Nizao; but when he understood that among other things Señor Delfino would probably receive by the Alice a *máquina* for pulling stumps out of the ground, as a dentist draws teeth, he was all alive to have a hand in the first experiment.

The only ground I had open to this work was the corner of the Home Field occupied by a part of the yuca crop, which I was at this very time taking out and delivering to Captain Ramirez on our old contract.

Felix volunteered his help to dig the yuca, as well as in operating the stump machine; and on its being accepted he started home directly from church in the morning, to get his working clothes and give some farm directions, in order to hasten back by Monday evening. While Juanico was absent at Bani I had commenced digging yuca with two hired men under charge of Juan, and fortunately that business was nearly over when Delfino arrived.

I have also had to make the rounds of my fruit-trees this month; pruning here, earthing up there, and leaving them clean about the roots everywhere; and this, with an hour's help and supervision in the yuca patch, pretty well carried away my forenoons for the first two weeks in October. There was plenty to do still before me, but now that I had Delfino with me the work went merrily on.

The men had to labor steadily in the yuca-field, for Captain Ramirez was impatient to get the crop to market. He made his account handsomely with the potatoes, and hoped to do quite as well with the yuca, but in this we were both somewhat disappointed.

The potatoes were in the main planted in the old clearing, where the ox-plough could be driven through the rich loam without much difficulty. A large portion of the yuca, on the contrary, was planted in the fresh clearing, where the plough could only meander among the stumps in a tediously imperfect manner, and where much of the work, from beginning to end, digging out the cróp included, had to be done in the slow, laborious, and unprofitable mode of the country, which is invariably by hand, with the heavy native hoes. The result is, that it cost me three times as much labor to get two hundred bushels of yuca out of this stumpy ground as it did to take up the same quantity of potatoes, where I could furrow them out with the plough. The yield is also fifty per cent. less to the acre; the roots not only being few in number, but small in size; and my gains on this part of my planting are very insignificant. This discouraging comparison only applies, however, to the acre and half, or thereabouts, dotted with stumps; the remainder of the yuca was on clear ground, and has made me as good returns as my corn and potatoes.

Felix came back in time to aid us in disposing of the last of the yuca, and every thing was made ready to welcome the "stump-extractor."

The Alice did not heave in sight until late Tuesday afternoon, and we had a busy day Wednesday getting Delfino's property ashore and housed. The stump-puller we set up at once on the field of operations, and gave it a hurried trial the same afternoon, but it was already late, and we were, besides, too tired to attack a stump of respectable size that evening.

On Thursday we mustered in full array, and after selecting a grand old logwood stump to start with, we all went at it with vigorous determination. Juanico hoed away the ground, to lay bare to the axe the large out-lying roots; I chopped them off, at a distance of two feet or thirty inches from the stem; Delfino adjusted the heavy chain-hooks to these prongs, and Juan, Felix, and a stalwart native plied the lever. Slowly, but surely, uprose the stump, "broadside to," until it rested on the tips of the set of prongs opposite to those held by the chains. Then we "slacked away," and carried the hooks close into the body of the stump for pull number two.

All hands now bent to the lever, for we were all excited with our splendid beginning, and eager to give it the crowning touch. The binding under-roots strained and snapped, the earth dropped away, and the gnarled and spreading net-work lay up-turned to the sun. Felix was in ecstasy; Delfino gave a long, glad shout, and I am sure I did my part towards swelling the hubbub of joy that welcomed the brave first effort of our new stump-machine.

In a short time several of our neighbors presented themselves, to look and talk merely, as they had flattered themselves, but, as we chose to interpret the situation, to work with us. We soon had them busy with hoe, axe, and lever. Delfino and I organized ourselves into a committee of direction; and when at dinner we revised our proceedings, and reported to each other in detail, we were unanimously of the opinion that we had performed our duties to admiration. Whenever a well-built, sinewy man entered the field, we invited him to try with us the magical powers of the lever, or (merely to show him how the whole thing was done) to spell Juan with the axe or Felix with the hoe. If he came mounted we borrowed his animal, and himself with it, to drag away the extracted roots which "impeded the free progress of the work." Nobody was spared, and there was no relaxation of effort in any department until about twenty stumps had been wrested from the bosom of mother earth.

Anita, who had been collecting the wherewith in honor of Delfino's company, contrived a rather neat collation, to which all who had held out till noon were invited. After the rest of the family and the strangers were dispatched, she gave us, that is, Delfino and myself, a mysterious hint to retire to the "North Arbor." This is an affair more shed than arbor, which Juanico and I had put up at odd hours against the rear of the cottage, for a kind of kitchen, and sleeping-place for an occasional hired hand. It is a retired nook, one side of which is covered with a fruit-yielding variety of the passion-flower, and Anita had now set it in order for a more elaborate dinner, which she had prepared for the *Señor Vecino y sus amigos nobles*—for me and my "noble friends."

I understand Anita's motives in securing me a little quiet and privacy at meal-time and looked round for Delfino. He had started off before me, and I stepped in after him to a most pleasant surprise. For Don Julio met me at the doorway with outstretched hand, and explained that he had cautioned Anita not to mention his arrival, until I had disposed of the men who had followed me from the field. He too had come to see the operation of the "Yankee Stump-Extractor," but he laughingly warned me not to expect much assistance from him; for he did not take kindly to axe, hoe, or lever; having in short a constitutional inaptness for all classes of useful employment.

Delfino replied that the *máquina* was a curiosity not to be exhibited or comprehended under the price of at least an hour's faithful service; still, out of tender consideration to his friend's chronic debility, moral and physical, which, he was sorry to admit, he knew was no pretence, but an affecting and incurable reality, the terms should be modified to meet his case. Don Julio would only be required to put to work and keep at work, whatever tenants of his own should happen to straggle in upon us during the afternoon.

"Will you not accept as a substitute my mayoral, who is coming over with a brace of hands and a yoke of oxen, to offer their assistance for a day or two?" inquired Don Julio, as he seated himself at the table, and held out his plate for some of Anita's appetizing chowder.

"By no means; I will prove to you that it is an absurd proposition, *amigo mio*," said Delfino, holding out his plate in turn. "Your mayoral, your servants and your oxen, must be considered as pupils, whom we shall favor *gratis* with a course of instruction in a new and profound branch of science. They ought to pay us liberally for teaching them, but we are generous, and will waive that, only insisting that you, who unfortunately have not the capacity to learn any thing useful, shall be kept out of mischief by at least 'playing work.'"

Anita put an end to this pleasant war of words by bringing in the roasted chicken, and with it a message from Juanico to the effect that Don Julio's people had come, and that Felix had already returned to the field with them, and that he, Juanico, was waiting my orders. I directed him to go on as in the forenoon, with axe and hoe, preparing the roots for the action of the *máquina* until we joined them. Delfino added a charge that every man who entered the field should forthwith be set to work, but that no one, not even Felix, should be permitted to use or meddle with the stump-machine until we were on the ground to direct its management. We then voted ourselves, after the fashion of managers, another hour of rest before we joined the laborers, and that brought us among them only when it was nearly three in the afternoon.

We found half the working men of Savana Grande, and a sprinkling of the women, assembled to witness proceedings, but few of them were allowed to be idle spectators. Those who had neither hoe nor axe to work with, were directed how to chop off the roots of the smaller stumps with their *machetes;* and those who could do nothing else were employed in prying up the points of the prongs the others had cut, thus putting them in greater readiness to receive the chain-hooks. Felix and Don Julio's old mayoral flew about the field like men possessed with the very demon of activity, giving no one a moment's respite, and really getting no small amount of hard work out of these forced recruits. The stump-machine was well plied that afternoon.

Delfino took the charge of that, with the serene pride of conscious power. He would, as a particular favor, call up by threes and fours the men who had been at work getting the roots in the proper state, and teach them practically, as part of the entertainment, how to use the lever. Now and then an obstinate old stager would cling to its long anchorage with especial tenacity, but we overcame them one by one as we went on, and left nothing behind us but one large and stubborn mahogany stump, not far from the corner.

This patriarch of the forest had been cut down

long before I bought the place, but its vast size and solid spreading roots were still too fresh and stout for our hand-power extractor. We did not waste much time on it, however, and the less, as we used that corner for piling up roots to dry for fuel. A little hill of stumps soon rose upon and around the mahogany giant as we held on in steady earnest for the rest of the week.

The machine had been warranted to clear half an acre a-day, if worked by two good men, but it falls considerably short of this with us, though we had hoe and axemen to cut off the main spreaders, and two, often four men to work the lever. In three days, with plenty of help and no bad weather to impede us, we had gone over but about an acre. However, it was thoroughly cleared, with the single exception of that royal old mahogany stump. It was curious to see how the ground was dimpled with fresh holes, as if it had passed through a severe visitation of the small-pox.

Delfino suggests planting Irish potatoes in these beds, in a peculiar method, which he says a friend of his has lately tried with success, not in chance holes, but in trenches made for the purpose. For the last three or four years this gentleman has in this manner raised all he wants for family use. A part of the ground lies over for this experiment, which properly belongs to November, but the rest of it had to go under the plough at once for a crop of field-peas.

Delfino's mule-cart carried off, at the close of the week, most of the various articles the Alice brought for him, but he left the stump-machine with me for a few days. He would not take it away while my work was unfinished; besides, he wished his intelligent and confidential man Isidro to remain with me to practise upon it, as he had formerly done with the plough, and thus fit himself to assist his master in teaching the other servants how to use and take care of it.

Delfino himself finally decided to remain with me on condition that I would return with him to his plantation, if only to pass Saturday and Sunday.

I had closed and settled my yuca engagement with Captain Ramirez; the field-peas could be, and were attended to during the balance of Delfino's stay; all the farm-work for October was well out of hand, and what remained to be done could very safely be left to my trusty Juanico; so I felt myself free to close October with a few days' delightful relaxation with my friend Delfino on his sugar plantation.

His servant Isidro was directed to follow us on foot at his leisure, and I mounted the fine horse on which he came, to make the first pleasure trip I have allowed myself since my arrival in Santo Domingo.

We had a charming ride through a lovely country, over the broad savannas and then up through the romantic hills that encircle the town and table-lands of San Cristoval. The balmy, delicious mornings of Santo Domingo are seldom marred by high winds or rain, and in the exhilaration of our dashing ride, on Delfino's swift, easy-paced horses, the air seemed more fragrant and invigorating than ever.

Delfino's place is charmingly situated on the crest of a commanding plateau and replete with country comforts. Every thing is home-like and I felt at home. We went over his large plantation watching, examining, noting, comparing, planning, and working, even as we had gone together over my wild little homestead, both of us full of improvement projects.

Delfino is sick and tired of the hoe husbandry of Santo Domingo, and is bent on introducing our labor-saving implements from the United States. With such a tedious, expensive, unsatisfactory mode of tilling the soil, I only wonder that any man has the courage to attempt it. The one thing for which it will answer is said to be coffee, and Delfino's coffee grove undoubtedly does pay very well indeed, for the soil and climate are favorable and it is judiciously tended. But as to his sugar-field it does not return him, acre for acre, as much by forty per cent. as I have made out of my corn, beans, and potatoes. Sugar-raising on a large scale, with the best implements of agriculture, and suitable means for extracting and refining it, is probably the most profitable crop in the world except cotton, in a good cotton region; but to a man with narrow, imperfect means, breadstuffs and field vegetables are by far the surest dependence. This much I have learned for a certainty from my visit at Delfino's plantation. I had thought so before, but on a close scrutiny of out-go and income, I now *know* by reliable facts and figures that our northern way of cultivation, applied to products which every farmer there understands, may be counted upon, acre for acre and man for man, for a yield quite equal to any average sugar-crop. It is the bounteous climate, which allows productions to go on all the year round, and insures a continued succession of crops, and not this or that pet product, which makes tropical farming so profitable. Sugar, cotton, coffee, and indigo, undoubtedly make rich returns, but so does every other crop that man demands for his daily use; and every one with health and energy to do a man's work, can be sure of earning more in his potato and corn field than the best hands can clear in sugar, on average years. Delfino and I examined this point carefully, and, though we differed at first, we both came at last positively to this conclusion.

CHAPTER XII.

NOVEMBER.

Finish my visit.—Delfino surprises me.—We both return to Palenque.—Expected important arrivals.—Anita.—Fishing-day.—"Yankee Charles, of Baltimore."—His history.—American newspapers.—The "Stranger's Rest."—All Saints' Day.—Favorable omen.—Improvise a bee-hive.—Arrival of agricultural implements.—All grievously disappointed.—Dishonesty of the "house" in New York.—A warning to buyers.—Juanico and his garlic-bed.—Visit from Manuel, the carpenter.—Furniture from my own mahogany grove.

RESISTING my own inclinations, as well as Delfino's kind importunities to prolong my stay at his charming plantation, I made ready to start for home at daybreak the first morning of November. There was no extra press of work before me, but there was a series of secondary matters that required my attention, each in its due order; and every man that has any thing whatever to do, knows how much he gains in ease of mind, body, and business by a steadfast care to always do the right thing at the right time.

At the first stir of the household, I arose and looked out in the gray of the morning for a parting glance at the wide prospect commanded by the large window of my bed-chamber. As my eye roved in the direction of the "sugar-house" I perceived Isidro leading forward three saddle-horses instead of the single one I had expected to see standing at the door for my use. Delfino stepped out to meet him, and as he did so he caught sight of me, and instantly his cheerful voice rang through the house, summoning "each and every sluggard bound for Palenque to present himself for breakfast;" a summons I lost no time in answering.

While dispatching our coffee and omelette, Delfino told me he had decided over-night to go back with me, as he expected letters by the Alice in reply to some he had written to Santo Domingo City, and that he also wished to see and try with me a mill for grinding arrow-root which Don Julio had ordered from New York.

He had heard of the arrival of two vessels from New York, through a friend from that city who had passed by his house the day before, and he therefore considered it more than probable that the arrow-root mill might even then be on its way to Palenque.

"And why did you not mention this before?" I asked, in surprise. "You know, Delfino, that I have a kind of interest in this machine, and that it cannot be operated until I set it up and teach some of Don Julio's men how to manage it."

"Precisely for that reason I did not speak of it. You would have shot off to Palenque Bay at the first word, and I did not choose to supply the powder for such a catastrophe," answered Delfino, lightly. "Julio and the machine can wait until we come, and the more calmly, as neither you nor Julio have such an immensity of arrow-root but that you can get through with it all before Christmas."

"But we also want to apply the mill to grinding yuca for cassava bread, and for making starch, and there is plenty of that ready now," I said.

"Never mind, we shall be in the midst of it all in

good time, especially if we hurry up our horses. The Alice will scarcely be due before to-day, and by noon we will be ready to receive her as she touches the landing."

We dispatched our early breakfast, and were on the road at sunrise. Our ride seaward, with the fresh and welcome breeze playing upon us all the way down the hill-slopes and across the green level of Savana Grande, was truly delightful.

We were at the entrance of the New Road, leading by my homestead to Palenque, before nine; and sending Isidro to the house to inform Juanico of our arrival, in time, as Delfino said, "to warn Anita to put forward her highest company flourishes for dinner," we rode leisurely along to the Bay.

It was "fishing-day" at Palenque, and we found half the men of the neighborhood there, either to help draw the seine or to buy fish, or traffic with Yankee Charles for his famous "pies, pastry, and ginger cordial, all made in first-rate American fashion."

The custom of fishing with the seine on a fixed

day of the week, and the establishment of Yankee Charles's house of entertainment, are both excellent institutions, and both have grown out of the opening of a direct cross-road from the great highway of the savannas to Port Palenque—now much used—in connection with the regular trips of the coasting-sloop Alice.

Many other coasters, and occasionally some larger craft from foreign ports, visit Palenque, and have done so for years, to take on board the freights of precious woods which are sent here to be shipped; but until the Alice became a regular trader, and could be relied on as a kind of express-boat to carry, at sure intervals, the lighter articles of home production and home necessity, no one about Palenque thought of raising any such small matter as a little corn or cassava for the Santo Domingo market.

Captain Ramirez opened this small but convenient boat-trade by coming regularly for my garden-stuff, together with any odd lots of satin-wood, or other chance freights that might offer in those intervals when the large planters and rich forest-owners had no employment for him. The working people on the prairies have availed themselves of this certainty of reaching a good market in Santo Domingo City, and getting back what they wanted through an intelligent trader like Ramirez, and they begin to learn the convenience of a good road for the conveyance of their stuff to and from the landing.

After this discovery on their part, I had but to set the day and lead the work, to insure a general meeting for road-making, whenever it was necessary to call the neighbors together for the purpose.

Neither were the great land-owners, whose domains touched the Bay, backward in sending men and teams to assist in repairing the road, after it became clear to them that this assistance was not thrown away. They saw that it was in effect a real enhancement to their broad but roadless and uncultivated estates, and some of them are now my fast friends and liberal encouragers in these local improvements.

One day there dropped down on the margin of Palenque Bay, how or from where I scarcely know, the keenest and readiest of Baltimore ship-stewards, in search of employment. He drifted in, like a waif of the sea, from a coasting craft, but was so taken with the beauties of the place, or with those of a dark damsel of the savanna, that he resolved to anchor there for life. He obtained permission to put up a cottage and fence in a snug garden at a low ground-rent, and took to himself the tidy little prairie-girl for a wife.

The pair soon became well known, and general favorites throughout the neighborhood.

Their neat cottage, in which the town proprietors, wood shippers, and coasting captains were certain to find cleanly and comfortable entertainment, enlarged itself into a *tienda*, at which fine wheaten rolls, nice cakes, and a superior cup of coffee were always to be had, with the addition of a plate of unrivalled fish-stew on the weekly "seine hauling."

Yankee Charles has made that day as gay and busy as a fair in Europe, by the variety and excellence of his accommodations, and people of all classes flock in to see the sport, and enjoy the splendid sea-bathing, and they often wind up with a lively dance in the evening.

Delfino and I rode up to his door without the intention of dismounting, but Charles met us, cap in hand, with such a polite invitation to come in and "try an oyster patty of American make," that we could do no less than accept it.

I had heard of oysters in the vicinity of the Nizao, but had never seen any, and was in truth rather doubtful of their existence until Charles set the veritable article before us. He conducted us to a new building which he had just erected in his garden, and which fronted the sea, "where," he said, "gentlemen could be private and read the papers, while he prepared any delicacy of the season they might choose to order."

This last crowning touch of civilization overcame Delfino, and he threw himself back in his chair for a long, hearty laugh, while Charles, at my request, produced his "latest American papers."

With a smile of calm triumph he laid before us a respectable lot of the weekly *Herald*, *Sun*, and

Sunday Dispatch, not very old, or, to express it with due fairness, quite recent in date, considering where we were. They were, at least, the latest I had seen, and I was soon busied in them to the neglect of the oyster patties and the other "delicacies," which Charles had laid so neatly before us. Ramirez brings me papers as they arrive from the States or St. Thomas, and Charles has made interest with him to obtain from the servants of the British and American Consulates all the spare newspapers as fast as their masters have done with them. He informed us that he subscribed himself for a Spanish literary monthly and the Santo Domingo Gazette, and these he respectfully proffered to Delfino.

Verily, none but a man trained in the school of Yankee enterprise would have attempted, or could have succeeded, in establishing such a "Stranger's Rest" as this colored Charles has built up on the shores of this delightful bay.

I feel a sympathy with his labors and successes, for they are not unlike my own single-handed battle, and, as in my case, his steady, earnest struggles for a sure resting-place have won him a pleasant and permanent homestead.

We lingered an hour over the "latest papers" and "oyster patties," and then, with one last sweeping, lingering scrutiny seaward, in the hope of detecting the sails of the Alice in the distance, we mounted our horses and rode rapidly home. Juanico was watching for us at the gate, and his whole face lighted up with honest joy at seeing us ride in, praising the order and freshness that reigned over the scene.

We gave our horses to Juanico and walked to the cottage through the fruit-grove, gathering as we went a few limes and an enormous "soursop," for our dinner beverage. Here a startling surprise arrested me. As I reached up to seize a branch, in order to bring the fruit within grasp. I observed a swarm of bees clustered on a limb above it, and hastily called to Delfino for instructions. He has scores of hives on his plantation, and takes much interest in the management of bees, but I had no idea he was such a practical adept.

He sent me with orders to the old cabin, where, laying hands on an empty half-barrel, for I had no box, or bits of board, to turn into a more regular hive, I bored four holes in the sides with the inch-bit, and passed through, and across each other, a couple of sticks from the nearest bush, wedged them in place, and carried this extemporized hive to Delfino under the tree. Meanwhile he had spread under it a table-cloth, which he had snatched from Anita's hands as she was about arranging for dinner, and was brushing the bees down upon it when I joined him. He had nothing over his face or on his hands, as he stood looking up at the broken and confused swarm, while he boldly brushed down the divided clusters. He laughed at my timidity, as I stood hesitating at a distance, and taking the barrel from my irresolute hands he laid it on the cloth, and continued driving the bees into it with a leafy twig until the main body had actually entered.

"The queen-bee has gone in, and her subjects are quietly exploring their new realm," said Delfino, peering into the capacious hive. "We may leave them now to make up their minds about settling in it, and go to dinner. Anita will have to find another table-cloth, however, for this must remain where it is until dark, when we can move the hive to its place."

Anita disposed of the question of table-cloth without difficulty, and she prophesied no end to the good fortune which an early swarm of bees, a swarm presented to me on All Saints' day, is infallibly to bring to my house. May her words prove true! I am not sanguine, though, on the subject of bees and honey, for I have no experience in bee-culture, but I shall manage my unexpected prize to the best of my ability.

In the afternoon I fitted up a bee-bench under the interlocking canopy of the old coffee-trees beyond the spring, and at dark Juanico, who I find has a perfect knowledge of bee husbandry, conveyed the barrel to its place. The busy tribe settled down to work, and in three weeks had nearly filled the upper third of their strange hive with clear, beautiful comb.

I have only looked at them this once, but I am getting up a decent stock of courage to encounter the first young swarm they may send out.

In this country, as almost everywhere in tropical

America, the bees have *two* seasons in the year instead of *one*, as at the North. In the early spring they lay up large quantities of honey, and swarm freely in May and June. Then they rest awhile from their labors, but resume them again in August. This second term of honey is, I am told, inferior to that of the spring season, but in November and December most of the swarms throw out two or three new ones; the young swarms of May and June vying with the older ones in the number and vigor of their colonies. Sometimes the winter swarming closes in January, and the bees take another period of rest during the balance of the dry season. They do not fail, however, to lay up more or less honey, and with the spring rains they recommence again.

Mine of the first of November were rather early in the season, but it is by no means a remarkable case. There is always some swarming early in November, though not on the extensive and prolific scale generally witnessed later in the month and throughout December.

This much for the bees, every word of which is,

however, borrowed from the lips of my friend Delfino, who promised, moreover, to instruct me in the art of making a medicinal cordial from honey and fresh ginger. How valuable it may be as a medicine, I cannot attest, but to its merits as a pleasant and palatable cordial I can bear witness, for I enjoyed it with uncommon zest while at his plantation.

The Alice came in late at night, and in the morning we went in force to the landing to take charge of the long-expected arrow-root mill. Don Julio met us there, as impatient as ourselves to see it in operation.

I was vexed to see that it had been shipped in a shamefully careless manner by the New York agricultural-warehouse firm, and I would fain publish the name of this concern, that others may learn not to trust its *guaranties*, when they boastfully announce, "that whoever orders any thing from their house may depend upon the superior quality of the articles, and also on the greatest care being taken to pack them suitably for transportation."

The mill for "grinding arrow-root, yuca, and other

bulbous roots," was in every respect a failure and a deceit, nor was it alone in this that we were disappointed.

A honey-press that came out with it for Don Julio, was so badly made that it broke the first day it was used, and was hopelessly past all service in a fortnight.

Happily for us, we were ignorant of the worst disappointments in store for us when we all met that morning at the Palenque landing, to welcome the first machines of their class ever seen in that district.

Reports had crept abroad that Don Julio and I had ordered from the North some *máquinas* of extraordinary power for grating yuca, and the whole population was on the *qui vive*, for that is a subject of universal interest here.

Yuca, grated very fine and thrown into water, settles at the bottom in a delicate flour which the natives bake into the thin cakes, called cassava, of which I have already spoken. This is the common bread of the country, and at present the grating is always done by hand; a slow, hard, unsatisfactory process for the women, on whom the labor chiefly falls. The plough, the weeder, the scythe, and the stump-extractor had created grand sensations, but the *máquina* that was "to do in one day the work of twenty women for a week," would eclipse all its predecessors, and there was a general voice of supplication from both sexes to see it set in operation at the earliest moment.

It was transported at once to Don Julio's place, with all its belongings, and set up in the room previously prepared for it. We had the intention of practising it a day or two before the public were admitted; but it was impossible to exclude a real mob of the curious "personal friends" of Don Julio. They would press into the room with troublesome proffers of help, or stand about in everybody's way while we were getting it in gear.

The first handful of yuca that was thrown into the hopper came out in coarse, half-ground "chunks," good for nothing but to send to the pigs. I set the mill to its finest capacity, but it turned out nothing that answered the splendid promises of the agricultural house on whose recommendation and guarantee it had been bought. We tried young arrow-root, hoping that the tender bulbs would yield us a more encouraging show, but all in vain. We tried all things in all ways, over and over again, until we were forced to give up the mill as a false pretence. I wasted an anxious, laborious week on it, in the vain hope that in some shape it could be made serviceable, but there was no good in it.

The poor neighbors felt the disappointment keenly, for they knew it was bought more for their use and instruction than for Don Julio's profit. He felt the annoyance of such a public failure far more than the loss of the money, and I felt it most deeply of all, perhaps, because it was ordered at my urgent recommendation, and I had rashly advised him to send for it on the statement of an agent of the house that this mill is like those used in the manufacture of the Bermuda arrow-root, which is simply a deliberate falsehood.

While I was at work at the mill, Juanico had to manage the homestead as best he could, but the faithful fellow went on diligently, and when I returned home late on Saturday night, sufficiently tired and disheartened, his warm welcome and pleasant account of home progress restored me to myself. Yet it required the lapse of one day of profound rest—the blessed, care-forgetting Sabbath, to wear off my mortification and bring me in trim for my homestead duties, and enable me to return with a cheerful spirit to my crops.

The November returns are not immense, but there are two hundred dollars for my corn from the New Field, with the likelihood of as much more in December from my other crops. I have to pay something for extra labor, but not much of it out of these field-crops. My garden beans, melons, onions, and other stuff, continue to return me nearly enough to meet my current expenses.

I had given Juanico, at his own request, the entire charge of a frightfully large garlic-bed, and he has tended it with such assiduity, that I have resolved to make over to him, for the purchase of a Christmas suit, that great pile of it which he is braiding into *ristas*, while I am writing. He is seated at the end of the garden walk, on guard over a grand heap of vegetables, the produce of our joint labors, and he eyes them from time to time with a loving glance while waiting for Captain Ramirez to call for them. He breaks into a whistle now and then as he braids his garlic tops, but always very softly, for fear of disturbing my occupation at the table, drawn outside the cottage door.

We have just set out most of our seedling plants, and my Winter Garden is stocked with young vegetables to begin the coming year. The rainy season is drawing to a close, and our work for this year is nearly done. To-morrow is Sunday, and the day after begins the holiday month of December, and I propose to commence it auspiciously by surprising Juanico with the wherewith for his Christmas outfit.

Last night Manuel, the carpenter, called for the money for making the doors and shutters of my cottage. I lived without them some months, but when I was so far prospered that I had means to spare, after buying a stout mule and a pair of young cows,

I engaged him to finish off my house. It was completed ten days ago, but since then he has made me a lounge and wardrobe of mahogany from my own ground, and now our simple home is ready for the dear friends for whose sake, not less than my own, I have been struggling to win a settled abiding-place.

CHAPTER XIII.

DECEMBER.

The ripening corn.—Hoe-husbandry.—Unbroken succession of crops.—Plans for the future.—Affectionate fidelity of Juanico.—Attempt to finish my cottage.—Dishonest mason.—Unlooked for disappointment.—What I resolve to do.—Juanico's proposition.—Felix comes to my relief.—The lime-burner.—Cottage finished.—Delfino appears suddenly.—What he insists on.—Preparations for a Christmas-tree.—Everybody to be invited.—Site selected.—The company assemble.—We celebrate Christmas joyously.

OCTOBER, November, and December are much the same thing in the records of a small Dominican homestead. The corn ripens in one or the other of these months, according as it is planted in July, August, or September.

I have but little to harvest this month, and not a great deal to plant. The ground assigned to my cocoa-nut grove was intended for a planting of pole-beans, and the original plan was in some degree carried out immediately on my return from Delfino's sugar plantation on the first of November. Between the lines of young cocoas, the ground is covered with long rows of bean-vines, whose fruit is destined for the Santo Domingo market, through the dry months of January, February, and March. The October and November plantings yield less foliage and come more slowly to maturity than those made in the pushing vigor of the three summer months; but with deep ploughing and one careful cleansing with the donkey-cultivator in the first weeks after they are above ground, corn, beans, and so forth, will return fair crops, and they have the advantage of coming into market in the season of no rains and high prices.

In this particular, the system of plough-culture produces a fabulous profit, while the shallow native hoe-husbandry returns nothing but a loss. Hoe-husbandry does not go deep enough to carry the tender, thirsting rootlets down to a moist bed, and the plant dries up and dies out in the long succession of sunny, rainless days. The plough and cultivator supply this vital necessity of moisture to the growing crop. They loosen the earth so as to enable it to drink in the heavy dews, and permit the searching rootlets to penetrate to the cool dampness of the subsoil, while the uprising of a gentle vapor, that is constantly disposed to ascend from a considerable depth, refreshes as with a bath the spreading fibres that are exploring the earth for this watery aliment.

While the hard, untilled, and consequently sun-scorched native fields around Palenque are being given up for the season, as too late for successful planting this fall, my ploughed land is covered, this last week of December, with crops of corn ripening for sale next month, and with patches of beans in every stage, from flowering to ripeness, with a promise of a continuous supply for the next two months.

I have aimed at a succession of crops, and, including garden vegetables, I have not failed in having something to sell from May to December.

With me it was an urgent necessity to obtain the quickest and closest series of vegetables and bread-stuffs which this genial climate will produce ; but on reviewing the year's work, month by month, I cannot but think that every planter, large or small, will find it more profitable, as well as more comfortable and independent, to give a wider range to his usual planting list, and devote somewhat more attention to raising within his own limits, all that is required for the consumption of his own homestead.

Coffee, *sugar*, *rice*, and *cotton* are precious staples, and make such brilliant returns that they dazzle the great proprietors, and wholly divert their attention from the sure and steady, though unpretending, profits of those crops that form the daily food of all classes.

Men must eat of many things besides sugar, coffee, and rice, and they must pay a fair price for them. The simple and inevitable result of this fact, as I have fully realized, is, that whoever chooses to raise food in this country may rely on a good demand and remunerative prices. The rich planters will not compete with him, because their thoughts and means are concentrated on the great staples for export; and the others cannot, for the small native farms are tilled under such a wretched, profitless system, and their owners are so trained to it, that they would have to be born again and live a new life before they could be taught to understand the labor-saving appliances of good husbandry.

In this climate of incessant production, every month ought to be made to bring with it some gainful harvest of fruit, vegetable, or breadstuff. From April to November the farmer can go on with a steady succession of plantings, and after the first year it will be his own fault if he does not have an equally steady succession of harvestings. This has been my experience. As I cleared the ground of the crops put in it during the early rains in April and May, I planted afresh for new returns in the dry months of the coming year.

With the later rains of October and November I have covered nearly every foot of my winter garden with ocra, onions, tomatoes, sugar-peas, radishes—in a word, with the round list of vegetables with which I started my seedling bed in January last. These are now thrifty, well-advanced plants, many in flower, and some beginning to bear, so that the coming January will be, as I may reasonably trust, a harvest month. My patient labor has been paid by the rapid advance of all my vegetables under the spring showers, and their readiness for early sale when the market was at its best. Now, with the advantage of the fall rains to give it a strong start, my winter garden stands a fair chance to give me three-fold profits with the same amount of labor.

My New Field will probably give me a cheering account of sweet potatoes in February and March, of yuca in April and May; and then I shall ask no more of it until I attend to my yautilia in August and September, unless, indeed, I plant early corn in the cocoa-nut grove. It is now ready for January, to gather in weekly supplies of lima-beans for Captain Ramirez. Should I plant that space in corn with the first rains next Spring, as Don Julio advises, it ought to supply the housewives of Santo Domingo City with young corn for *arapa* in June and July, and thus keep up a regular course of crops and employment from January to September.

After these will present themselves, one after the other, in October, November, and December, the spring and summer planted crops, and so complete the circle of monthly harvests for the entire year.

I believe I can rely on Juanico and the winter garden for the support of the house, including his own wages and those of one or two men a part of the time.

Juanico himself is henceforth to be counted a fixture of the homestead. In squaring our accounts, he supplicated me not to speak of formal wages, but to keep him always by me, and to take care of him as long as he lives. He is the most patiently industrious Dominican I have yet seen, and by no means wanting in the capacity to learn and appreciate the use of improved implements of agriculture. His nature is single-minded, docile, and faithfully affectionate, and he is prized by me rather as an humble friend than a paid servant. This, however, does not change my resolution to give him the usual Dominican wages; three dollars a week to men who live in the house. Beyond that, I consider from time to time his little extra personal wants, and take care of them as liberally as my means will admit, if only to manifest my sense of the value of his services.

In the first half of December we set ourselves zealously at the work of plastering and whitewashing our palenca walls. There was some trouble about the lime, as well as with the native mason who had contracted to supply it and do the plastering. After the prices were arranged, and the day fixed for beginning, he changed his mind, and refused to undertake the job unless I would promise to add another five dollars to the sum first agreed on, twenty dollars, and advance him ten dollars "to pay a debt that troubled" him. Here was a dilemma. Twenty dollars was the full value of the work, and I dislike to yield to unjust and arbitrary demands; but, on the other hand, I was exceedingly anxious to have the house finished, and all the rubbish cleared up before Christmas, for Delfino had written to say that he would be with us on Christmas Eve, and he particularly claimed "a week of free and perfect holiday, at the close of my first year's trial of *life in Santo Domingo*."

The mason called in person to inform me of his rise in price, and to take home with him the ten dollars advance, for it did not occur to him that I had any choice in the matter. I had stipulated so strongly to have the work completed at least ten days before Christmas, that he evidently supposed I would submit to any exaction rather than be disappointed. He was the only mason within five miles, and the only lime-burner was his own cousin, and, for aught I knew, this cousin might refuse to sell me the lime I needed. The exceeding desire I felt to have my cottage plastered and regulated before the close of the year, caused me to waver a moment. As I looked up with the intention of offering to "split the difference," I caught such a leer of triumph in the fellow's eye, that I instantly resolved to have nothing more to do with him.

"As you find the bargain we made so much to your disadvantage, I will let the house stand as it is for the present," I said, composedly. "The weather is now settled, and I can do very well in it for the four months of the dry season, since it has answered

13

perfectly through all our rains. Consider our engagements, therefore, absolutely at an end."

The man was taken aback; I saw *that* at a glance, and this quite reconciled me to my own disappointment.

"But about the lime, Señor? That must be taken, for it is engaged," he observed, after a few minutes of awkward silence. "I bespoke it on my own responsibility for this particular work. Two cargoes of lime are to be delivered here this very day, at a dollar a barrel, and my cousin expects the money for it from your hand." He paused and looked at me for an answer, but I did not speak. I was reflecting on the "situation."

"You consented to that and to the price," continued he, in an insolent tone.

"Certainly I did, but it was a part of my arrangement with you," I answered; my own temper calming in proportion as his rose. "You do not choose to abide by the rest of the bargain, and of course I shall not take the lime."

There was another pause, which the mason at length

broke by proposing to abate two dollars from his price, if I would advance the ten dollars and receive and pay for the lime when it came.

"The exact bargain, or nothing. No advance, and half a dollar deducted for every day the work is delayed beyond the time named for its completion," I answered, decidedly.

"No money until *all* the work is done?" interrogated the man, in a tone of surprise, as if that was a new condition, though it had been made a leading stipulation, because I had been told that there is no other way of getting these people to keep on witn their work until it is completed.

"No payment for my work until it is every bit finished?" repeated the man, in an injured, querulous tone.

"No."

"Then, I must warn the Señor that no Dominican can be found who will work for him. *Adios!*"

Away he went, in a state of high fermentation at the general upsetting of his plans.

I too had my own feeling of discomfort at this misunderstanding. It is the first I have had in this country, and I would gladly hope it may be the last, but I could not consent to yield to these petty extortions; I would sooner let the cottage wait a year.

But it did not have to wait a day. When I rejoined Juanico at our work on the Winter Garden, I dropped a word or two of regret that the cottage should remain unplastered for months to come, and not be put in the condition to receive Don Delfino which we had anticipated.

"If you wish the work done, Señor, I will go over to Nizao and capture another mason directly," said Juanico, quietly, without raising his eyes from his tomato gathering, or relaxing the speed of his busy hands.

"Do you really think you can find a mason at Nizao, Juanico?"

"I have no doubt of it, Señor; but if I fail there, I will step over to Bani (the *step* to Bani is only fourteen miles) and bring you Felix," replied Juanico, this time looking up eagerly and speaking with animation.

"Is Felix a mason, then?"

"Si Señor. His father was the best mason in this part of the country, and Felix worked with him until he died, three or four years ago. After that, Felix left his trade because he liked farming better. But he will come to you flying when he knows you need his services."

"I would be truly glad to have him, and you may take the mule and ride over to Bani as soon as you like, Juanico, to propose it to him, and to inquire how we are to get the necessary lime."

"As to the lime, it has settled itself," said Juanico, putting down his tomato basket and starting towards the New Road. "Somebody is calling at the gate, and I can see from here two donkeys with white loads."

Juanico had hit the truth, and he and the lime-burner had a long parley, which I was not slow to conjecture was about the mason's breach of contract. Before they were through with it, Juanico had wormed out of him that the lime was really sold for eighty cents, instead of a dollar, the barrel; and at this lower price the donkeys were led in to discharge their loads. The other materials were on hand and in their place, so that the only remaining difficulty was to learn whether we could secure a mason in time to get through before Christmas.

Juanico rode over to Bani in the evening, and before ten the next morning Felix solved the doubt by presenting himself with an assistant. In a word, matters were driven with such energy that every thing was finished, every sign of mortar and building trash cleared off, outside and in, and the cottage put in its trimmest order on the 20th, four full days before Christmas.

While we were in the midst of our labors, the original contractor sent to say that, "not to fail in his word, and for the pleasure of obliging a neighbor like me, he would undertake the work on the terms first proposed; but that he could not limit himself by a promise to have it done before Christmas."

I returned thanks for his kind intentions, and sent answer that, as the job was already nearly finished, I had no occasion for his services.

My white cottage gleams cheerfully through the green foliage of the over-arching trees, and I am most happy in its possession.

I slept a week in the old cabin while the plastering dried, and we were not through a day too soon, for Delfino—God bless him and his evermore—rode in on Saturday evening, attended by his man Isidro, with a mule-load of well-chosen and welcome gifts. Always the same sunbright and joy-giving spirit is Delfino.

"*Amigo mio*, I have come to take full and absolute possession of you and your house, of your man-servants and your maid-servants, and of all that is within your gates!" he exclaimed, almost before he reined up his horse. "Let no one presume to work or be serious in my presence, while this year lasts. Hear and obey this edict, all ye who hope to live."

"Your sovereign pleasure, great potentate, shall be our law! and obedience will be all the easier, since your presence makes every day a festival with us."

"I am delighted to find my subjects in such a happy mood, and so well housed too," exclaimed Delfino, looking round the now white walls of my cottage. "I can scarcely believe this is our blessed old homestead, where we learned to plough and mow, like real Yankees."

"And where we taught the natives to chop down trees with Yankee axes, and draw out stumps with Yankee extractors," I added.

"Yes, *mi amigo*, yes. Lo, we worked like Yankees, and lived like Spartans, and enjoyed ourselves like Athenians. Is it not so?"

"I can answer for myself, Delfino, that I have been happy in my labors, and found my Spartan fare quite endurable when you were here to partake of it with me. Anita, I see, has prepared something this evening, and it may be as acceptable after your ride as we used to find it after our work."

After supper we sat awhile in the soft starlight, and chatted of the year's doings, and of the result of twelve months' experience in tropical farming, until Delfino broke the chain of conversation by the abrupt observation :—

"We must have a Christmas-tree for all the people who have worked with us. Oh, you need not question me with your eyes, as if to ask whether I have the slightest idea what I am talking about. We must have a Christmas-tree, I say. Not the artificial in-door affair of your cold northern climate, but a green, living, fruit-loaded tree, standing out openly in the pleasant air of our summer land, only it must be trimmed with garlands and hung with suitable presents for those who have a claim to be remembered by us."

"What a charming suggestion! I will do my utmost to help carry it out."

"Good. Then we have only to select the place and think of the entertainment. Not one of those who have worked with us is to be omitted."

"Right. Every one of them, with their wives and children, shall be invited. Juan and Anita shall take care of that."

In the morning, after an out-of-door breakfast, under the close, green shade of our favorite fruit grove, we leisurely made our rounds and visited the successive plantings and improvements of the homestead with loving interest.

The Orange Walk is still in its infancy, but my young grafted trees are growing thriftily amid a showy range of sun-flowers, planted to define the line and provide a change of diet, now and then, for my nice brood of chickens.

The little trees of the mango avenue have cotton plants between them, but they are hardly beginning to blossom as yet. This cherished avenue would be the least striking of my improvements, did not a low hedge of lilies and other flowering plants, already rich in bloom, redeem its present insignificance.

From that we passed into the New Field, to see the cocoa-nut grove (that is to be), and found the triple line of sprouts in fine order. Many of them are three feet high, and most of them are at least two feet above the ground. They each received a careful hoeing from my own hands, about a month after they were planted, and will require the same attention some time in February or March, and once again during the rainy season, and this is all that is strictly necessary to insure the well-being of these valuable trees.

The plantain walk has made the most astonishing progress of all. The great green leaves of those set out in June now almost meet overhead, and even those planted in August are four and five feet high. Delfino says that seven or eight months hence I may begin to have a regular supply of plantains and bananas, and from that time forward there will be every week fresh clusters coming on, in continually increased abundance.

Early on Monday morning we selected our Christmas-tree, a thrifty guava, encircled by other fruit-trees of larger growth and denser shade. It is a little beyond the spring, just where the sweep of coffee, wild plum, and pomegranate trees mingle their shrubby hedge with the loftier growth of the grand old fruit grove. There is plenty of soft grass under foot and cool shade overhead. There is pure water close at hand, and two limes near by loaded with golden fruit, to make our cool and wholesome beverage. Delfino says Nature arranged the site expressly for the Christmas festivals of a man who is learning how to live in the primitive content in which Columbus found the first lords of this lovely island.

Our preparations were truly Arcadian. The trees around supplied the fruits; our viands were, to the last item, home-grown and home-made, and our beverages—mead, coffee, lemonade, native wines, and chocolate at the close of the day (after the presents were distributed)—were produced, without a single exception, on my own place, or brought from Delfino's sugar plantation. Yet our forty guests, men, women, and children, found no lack of wholesome and palatable variety at our rustic banquet beside the Christmas-tree.

Never have I enjoyed a day of purer delight than this which I have passed on my own honestly earned homestead, entertaining with hospitable care those who, in direct labor or neighborly kindness, have served me so well during the twelve months now concluded. They have done much to aid me in my new life, and I fervently pray that another year may again gather us all together under the richly laden boughs of our next Dominican Christmas-tree.

CHAPTER XIV.

BY WAY OF EXPLANATION.

HUNDREDS of the working classes are seeking new homes in countries where *intelligent* labor can best be made to supply the want of capital.

The unhealthiness of certain commercial sites has created a popular idea, that all tropical countries are necessarily unfavorable to health. This is a great mistake; not only are many of the high and well-drained table-lands of the tropics eminently healthy, but they are beyond dispute those regions in which men who know how to work with the best implements of agriculture, and who have the will to use them, are most certain to achieve an early independence.

In these favored regions of perpetual production, a man works only for his own profit and the embellishment of his home; while, in the land of long frosts, half of his labors are swallowed up in the service of that unrelenting, unproducing despot—Winter.

It becomes thus far a question of serious consideration, to a mechanic or farmer of limited means, where and how he may best secure a safe, pleasant, and independent homestead, in a land where snow and ice do not reign half the year, to devour most of the earnings of the summer.

I have endeavored to answer this question, by keeping from month to month an accurate diary of what I myself accomplished during one year in Santo Domingo, almost without any other capital than the labor of my own hands.

This diary has been written from time to time as my work went on. I have carefully given to each season of the year its own peculiar duties, together with the results of my actual experience. So far as it goes, I can safely declare it may be relied on by the emigrant to any part of tropical America, although the practical observations were made on the south coast of Spanish Hayti. This magnificent island—the favorite of Columbus—is, as the reader is aware, next adjoining Cuba, and, of all the West India group, nearest approaching that island in size, climate, and varied extent of its products. It is now under the Spanish rule, and possesses guarantees of personal liberty, to subjects and aliens, white and black, that cannot be questioned or set aside by any future rulers under the Spanish Crown, as these guarantees form part of the conditions of its annexation.

In conclusion, I may be permitted to say that, as a poor man, I decided to seek a home in a tropical climate, for three reasons:

1. In a climate of perpetual summer my labor would procure me a much larger variety, and a more continued succession of fruits, vegetables, and general comforts, than the same amount of work would command in a cold climate.

2. I knew I could create the necessary buildings for shelter, as well as provide needful clothing for my family the year round, with much smaller means in a climate without winter.

3. I could continue my work progressively the

whole year, without being brought to a stand still, for from one-third to one-half of the circle of twelve months, by the frost-locked earth. Thus, I could allow myself a remission from out-door work, at least one-third of the laboring hours of every day. I knew I could allow myself three hours of the noon-day, at least, for relaxation, for reading, or lighter employments in the cool house-shade, and yet at the end of the year, or a series of years, I should have accomplished as much in cultivating and improving my homestead, as I could have done at the North by working hard all the time. One-third of a farmer's time in the North is consumed in providing extra food and shelter for man and beast during the hard, *unproducing* winter.

Every month I have passed within the tropics has confirmed and deepened my certain knowledge of the superior advantages of a summer climate, for a working farmer of narrow means, especially if he labors systematically and with intelligence.

For myself I can truly say, although my life has been in a degree solitary, that the past year has been the happiest of my existence. In a few weeks I hope to welcome my dear brother and his two sons. This will afford me the companionship and society of my own race and kindred, the want of which is positively the only drawback I have experienced during my residence in this beautiful island.

THE END.

www.ingramcontent.com/pod-product-compliance
Lightning Source LLC
LaVergne TN
LVHW020238110826
845151LV00003B/959

* 9 7 8 1 4 2 5 5 3 0 1 3 6 *